My Precious Shepherd

(Psalm 23:1–2)

VOLUME I
THE LORD IS MY SHEPHERD SERIES

MARYWINN R. LENT

ISBN 978-1-64079-044-5 (Paperback)
ISBN 978-1-64079-045-2 (Digital)

Christian Faith Publishing, Inc.
296 Chestnut Street
Meadville, PA 16335
www.christianfaithpublishing.com

Cover chalk artist is Marywinn R. Lent

Printed in the United States of America

I desire to dedicate this book first to my loving husband who has graciously spent the last fifty years of his life together with me. Thank you for giving me the time to spend in this specific calling from our Lord Jesus Christ. I could not have written this book without your untiring support and encouragement.

Also, I want to dedicate this book to all of our children and grandchildren whether biological or *adopted in our heart.*

First of all, to our biological children, their spouses, and grandchildren:
Eddie and Birgit with Emily, Tabea, and Samuel.
Deena and Charles with James, Andrew, Christina, Marissa, Lydia, and Nathaniel.
David and Katrina with Daniel, Arianna, and Felicity.
Rachel and Todd with Savannah, Sterling, Morgan, Adele, and Gwinnett.
And Michael, who is single.

Secondly, to our loving Russian children, their spouses, and grandchildren who God called us to raise:
Nastya and Edvard with Vlada and Seva.
Katya with Varya and Dasha.
Pasha
Sveta

Thirdly, to our sweet Liberian daughter, her spouse, and grand-children that God in His sovereignty placed in our lives: Camolyn and Gerald with Manasseh and Madolyn.

Fourthly, to our precious Filipino friends that God has placed in our lives who have now become like our own precious family: Corey and Rina with Chole.

We are so proud of our entire family, whether biological or *adopted in our heart*. We love you all very much!

When our children were married, my husband and I had some teaching on *blessing* our children. George, had a part in each of their marriage ceremonies. He asked God to bless them with many off-spring among other things. God honored this request and 23 grand-children emerged over the years.

Thank you to Happy Jack Graphics that put my pictures in high resolution, Carriad Photography for taking cover pictures, and Tracy McCoy with the Georgia Mountain Laurel Magazine for her encouragement, wisdom, and input in the direction for this book.

PROLOGUE

I graduated from Savannah High School in 1963. Considering studying in several institutions of higher learning on my quest to attain a B.S in Education with a major in Speech Pathology, I graduated from the University of Georgia. After marrying George Lent in December 1966, we moved to Hilton Head Island, South Carolina where George was the first veterinarian in June 1967.

While living there, God used us to work in a new, small church. We had recently joined this church in the first few Sundays of it becoming an established congregation. Following two years, the pastor left abruptly. This left George in a position of heading this congregation while he was still young in the Lord. This church later became Grace Community Church and is a vibrant, mission minded congregation that is moving forward for the Lord today.

A few years later, God gave us the original vision for Hilton Head Christian School. God had laid this thought in our mind 2 years before this time, but our pastor said "No!" When we returned from Bible School, God provided a head master and one teacher. This school began in September 1979. Many other people were pioneers with us in this endeavor. This facility, several years later, became Hilton Head Christian Academy. Subsequently starting out with only 12 students, this school has become the home of nearly four-hundred students today.

After remaining on Hilton Head for 18 years, God has led us to a farm in the North Georgia mountains where we have lived for 31 years.

We have five children. Our 17 grandchildren are from our first 4 children that are married. Our last child remains single.

Then moving in 1986 to the mountains, God later called us to Russia for two years in 1994-96. We were in charge of five Russian orphans who lived with us in our apartment as if they were their own children. While in Russia and afterward, we brought these children home with us to our farm. We spent two complete school years in Russia and for nine summers the children came to us here in the states for three months. These children have been adopted in our heart. At present, we have four Russian grandchildren. We have remained in vital contact with them over these years.

Russia, also, brought us in contact with our Liberian daughter who is adopted in our heart also. She lived with us for five years while she was in college. She now is married and they have two children of their own. They, too, are our grandchildren.

Why did I write this book?

God urged me to begin writing this book three years prior. It was very hard to begin. God had to spiritually encourage me to lean totally on Him for this endeavor. He set me in His Word every day to discover His truths, and to memorize them. Furthermore, "For the Lord takes pleasure in His people, He will beautify the humble with salvation. Let the saints be joyful in glory; Let them sing aloud on their beds. Let the high praises of God be in their mouth, and a two-edged sword in their hand" (Psalm 149:4–6).

When we concentrate on who God is and what He has done for us, and memorize these verses about praise, our faith will be increased. This will cause us to realize what a mighty God we serve! That is what transformed me to be able to lean completely on God alone.

When I was in a spiritual position of completely trusting God to flow His wisdom and understanding through me, He used me to write this book. This is how God burdened my heart with His understanding:

1. I believe God wants us to *shape the next generation* because He has given us our children and allowed us to influence these Russian children, and a Liberian daughter. We now have twenty-three grandchildren through all of them. Since God has blessed us so mightily in these areas, He has given us a burden for the next generation.

2. Also, our children and grandchildren have expressed a desire to have *these stories to hand down to their children and grandchildren.* My desire is to make God real in the life of this family, and to show all people everywhere that God is alive and well in a very mighty way.

3. I desire *to make God real to others* so that they will see what a mighty God we have. God has made it plain to me that He will reveal Himself to all who will believe in and obey His Word (John 14:15–21). He will manifest or reveal Himself when we spend time each day in His presence by entering by prayer into the Holiest of Holies where the Almighty dwells. He desires for each one of His children to come to meet with Him before they start their day in this world.

4. Since God has allowed many trials that He has brought us through in life, He wants us *to proclaim His glory to all people.* My desire is that this book would reach all parts of the world for His glory to plant and water seeds, and bring in a spiritual harvest for His kingdom.

5. My prayer is that this book would be part of God's fireball *to turn the hearts of Christians and non-Christians to know God* in a deeper way. God has expressed that He is a consuming fire (Hebrews 12:29) and that He desires to sweep through His children and to cleanse them of their sins whether secret or outward (2 Chronicles 7:14).

God's refining furnace will set us on fire so that we will illuminate to others God's grace, mercy, and love.

6.   God has made Himself so very plain to me in my life as well as our life together. We have seen His Hand working for us, with us, to us, and in us. All of God's children must *be spiritually alert to recognize the twinkles from God* in everyday life. My prayer is that this book will encourage, enable, and enlighten everyone.

7.   God desires that His children would *walk in the power of His Holy Spirit*. If we truly have the power of the Holy Spirit of God moving in us, we will have a desire to witness to others. The power the apostles received at Pentecost caused them to go and tell others about Jesus. Three thousand were saved immediately after they received this power (Power promised—Acts 1:8; Power received—Acts 2).

Luke 4:18 is every Christian's commission on earth. How we carry out this will be different for all people. Allow God to show you how He wants you to carry out this commission and to bring much fruit into His kingdom (John 15).

This book is designed to be used best as a devotional, Bible study book. I desire that you read it slowly and consider what is being said, and then, you need to evaluate how God is affecting your life possibly in a similar way. Ask yourself questions to discover the hand of God in your life. Consider the questions found on pages 236-237. This is not a book to be read quickly in one sitting. I want you to reflect and write stories from your life as I have done. This is the first volume of a three-volume series. The progression of these books will be called *The Lord is My Shepherd Series.*

My Precious Shepherd includes stories of our life beginning when we met and started our family centered on Psalm 23:1-2. The second volume will be organized around our childhood years and more of our years together in verses 3-4, and likewise, the third volume will be based on our time in Russia, Krygyzstan, the Hilton Head Christian School, and other heart-warming stories of our life in verses 5-6.

I plan to write other series with stories from any ones' life. If you have a noteworthy story, please contact me at MyPreciousSheperd@ tutanota.com. I would love to possibly use your story in a future series.

CONTENTS

CHAPTER 1

The Lord is my shepherd Psalm 23:1a

What does a shepherd do?

1. A shepherd leads his flock. He goes before them. He does not push his sheep, but he gently leads them. The sheep knows the voice of their shepherd. He knows his sheep (John 10:3–4, 14–16).

2. He is always there to help his sheep. He never leaves his responsibility (Deuteronomy 31:6–8 and Hebrews 13:5).

3. He cares for and protects his helpless sheep (1 Peter 5:7).

4. At night, the shepherd is at the door of the sheepfold. No wild animal will get the sheep because he sleeps in the doorway. The good shepherd gives his life for the sheep (John 10:7, 9, 11, 15).

5. The shepherds break the self-will of the rebellious sheep (Isaiah 57:17d–18).

6. He heals their wounds and nurses them back to health (Luke 4:18, Jeremiah 17:14).

7. He leads them to better fields when provisions for food become scarce (Isaiah 48:17).

You are worthy, O Lord, to receive glory and honor and power; for You created all things and by Your will they exist and were created. (Revelation 4:11)

Worthy is the Lamb who was slain to receive power and riches and wisdom and strength and honor and glory and blessing! (Revelation 5:12)

1

Life is an Exhilarating Whirlwind!

This picture was taken in the early spring of 1963
when I was a senior at Savannah High School.

Life in all of its glory is extremely exciting at times! It is so wonderful to be needed and realize that you have a wonderful opportunity when you influence the life of others in a positive way. *How exhilarating!* Since God has blessed us with twenty-three grandchildren, I believe that He would have me to be involved with influencing them and others in this next generation for His glory. Praise His name!

When our first few grandchildren were very young, I started praying that God would allow me to be able to speak into their lives in many ways. He answered several years later. Because He has allowed us to be so very blessed with many young people in our family, I knew that God wanted me to find a ministry to help them discover who He really is.

The Lord had led me in the fall of 2005 to start a new program of homeschooling with three of our grandchildren and four students from the community. At the beginning of that fall, I was teaching them alone and realized a *great* need for a helper, especially since my age was increasing and their energy level would reach new heights every day.

As the school grew in student numbers, the school year of 2009–2010 was the height of the best years of my homeschool. There were fifteen children ranging from four to thirteen years of age, two helpers, and myself. By this time, more of our grandchildren as well as others in the community were coming into this program. Using my degree in education, my helpers and I were exploring many avenues in order to teach in exciting ways about secular events, subjects of every kind, and how each of these categories related to the Word of God. It was extremely exciting to me about what we were doing!

Oh, boy, what a utopian life! Each new day had it heights, but at the same time, this was extremely challenging and stressful to me to keep each grade on target at the same time. So my level of activity and emotional pressure increased greatly, but also, more helpers were added. Other than being massively busy and at times overwhelmed with stress, my life was going well, and it was extremely fulfilling. There wasn't any reason to think that *something is coming!*

In March 2010 through the rest of the year, my family and I had many opportunities to rejoice in the Lord, count it all joy, and pray without ceasing! At first, I had been having issues and trouble with my intestinal tract, specifically with my stomach, which were always looming in the background. Also, minor foot surgery was performed in February to help me walk more comfortably. Shortly after that in March, our youngest son lost consciousness during the school day and was rushed to Northeast Georgia Medical Center where several tests were performed; also, my husband had hernia surgery that May. Furthermore, there were pressures at church that were becoming overpowering, considering all these other issues.

After school was out in May, I began to be plagued with another major health obstacle. Since I had an injury to my back because of a chair being snatched out from under me as a young teen, I have had major issues with my lower spinal column. It continued until I was almost not able to sit very long or walk erect on rising. In the past, I have had two surgeries to correct a condition that was caused by the severe injury to my pelvis and lumbar spine. In order to obtain relief from the pain, I had to commence a series of injections in my lower spine. These injections were performed several times starting in April. I could not understand how I would be able to teach that fall, *but God!* Yes, but God intervened, and those injections relieved this condition enough to resume school in the fall.

This was only the beginning of our trials, and then the bottom dropped out of our slightly ruffled family nest. At times, I was wondering why so many trials came at once. Then I remembered a former pastor of mine said, "Good and bad run on parallel tracts, and they usually arrive at the same time!" Since school was the most fruitful element of my life at that time, I should not have been shocked when I was blindsided with other negative problems that would hinder my success.

Besides those problems, my stomach issues were becoming a *mountain* in my life. By this time, I could not eat anything except a small baked potato three times daily. Whenever I would try to eat additional foods, I would have dire results. Because of this, I made an appointment with my doctor so that he could re-evaluate this condition.

A gastrointestinal scope was performed in July 2010. The doctor reported that day that I did not have a hiatal hernia. I was so taken back because it had been diagnosed twice before several years apart. I did not say anything to the doctor, but George and I discussed this on the way home. The last report had reported that this hernia was increasing in size and severity.

Two days later, I saw the original doctor that had referred me to the one that had carried out the scope. He ordered a barium study of my esophagus and stomach area. This test revealed that not only had the hiatal hernia increased to greater proportions, but a diverticulum had formed radiating from my esophagus allowing food to be trapped there and never reaching my stomach. Hence, I was not receiving the nutrition from this food. Eating potatoes lasted for 8 months with increasing symptoms of pain, and nausea.

After having this recent barium study, we realized that the doctor that told me that I did not have this hernia was not being truthful to me. With these increasing symptoms, I investigated the possibility of having the surgery to remedy my hernia. Because, I did not have good insurance at this time, a certain hospital required that I pay them $25,000.00 in cash when I came to have this surgery.

This was far above our financial capabilities at that time. In October, I would qualify for a better insurance policy since my age was increasing. Furthermore, other tests had already been delayed due to several reasons.

Every time my mammogram was due, I refrained from having it for three years. The first reason for not having this test was because of being so very busy with school. Secondly, we did not have any insurance during those years, so medical facilities would require a sizeable deposit before they would arrange for these tests.

Meanwhile, my next birthday qualified me for a decent insurance plan. Oh, for joy! It was instituted on October 1, 2010, so all the criteria for several procedures were gathered at once. The first procedure was a colonoscopy on October 1; next, on October 5, as we were starting to head down to Atlanta for surgery the next morning, I stopped at my church to announce that I wanted to be in the Christmas play that year. I was given my part, and away we went toward Atlanta. On October 6, I had hiatal hernia surgery at Emory, which set me on a course that would result in me being able to eat again in several weeks. I had not eaten in more than nine months, except for eating a mashed potato three times daily. That was all I could hold down. What a busy and overwhelming several weeks! What will happen next! Oh, well, this is life, every golden minute of it!

Every time I completed one project, I checked it off my list of procedures for another year. Thank you, God! My mammogram was accomplished on October 13, and on the next morning, the center called to inform me that further testing was required. This was accomplished one week later along with an ultrasound.

At six-thirty in the afternoon of the same day, my gynecologist called to report that the radiologist said that I had cancer of the mammary glands in the left breast. This alarmed me greatly because, usually, being so definite about the fact that it was cancer without a biopsy was terrifying. I thought that it must be severe if they were able to be so definite without gathering all the facts first. By looking at the tests and the size of the tumor, I was told that I was possibly at stage two or three with breast cancer.

My doctor recommended a certain surgeon, but I was alarmed by a previous circumstance with that particular doctor, so I wanted to change to another surgeon. This surgeon had actually not been truthful with me about my hiatal hernia that began to develop after the birth of our first child. Because of this, I did not want him. I discussed with my husband as to which surgeon I should pursue. Since my gynecologist had gone out of town for the week, I could no longer discuss this with him. I felt alone and confused about how we were going to come up with another surgeon.

"Lord! What do you want me to do? I do not know how I am going to find a surgeon without my physician's help!" I literally *cried out* to the Lord! I was desperate to receive an answer from God. During that night, God awoke me at four o'clock in the morning. I knelt at my couch and prayed that God would show me what to do. An hour went by with frantic prayers, and then God filled me with total peace, so I returned to bed and slept soundly after that.

The next morning, as usual, I "chauffeured" my grandchildren to school. All the other children arrived at school on time, and all promptly commenced to study quietly. In my spirit, I was praising God and resting in the peace of the Lord that *something good is coming my way!*

At nine o'clock that morning, my husband called to report that he had found a surgeon. My first question was "How many weeks away is the appointment?" Then he told me that it was *that day* at two o'clock. "This *had* to be the hand of God!" I shouted! Now I ask you: "How many people are able to get an appointment with a doctor *that day?*"

My husband began explaining that we had to hurry in order for us to gather all the mammogram and ultrasound results and to be at the surgeon's office at the proper time. I also had to make arrangements for a teacher to come in and take my place for the rest of the day at school. I made one call, and God provided that teacher. Praise His name!

On the way to the doctor's office, I prayed that God would lead me to the doctor of His choosing. When my husband made the appointment, the receptionist revealed the name of my doctor I had previously visited. By the time, I arrived at the office, this staff reported to me that they had switched me to another doctor due to the fact that my first doctor was going to be out of town for the next week and was not readily available. The original doctor concluded he was not confident, that it was advantageous for me to wait for him to return. I was thrilled because I knew that truly God had chosen this particular doctor just for me! I believe that the Lord moved in a very special way on my behalf about which doctor to choose. I rested on this decision and was not anxious about switching doctors.

At that appointment on October 27, I was given a biopsy and ultrasound to determine exactly what kind of cancer with which we were dealing. On November 3, the results of the biopsy were revealed.

These results were horribly disturbing! I thought that God would be taking me home to be with Him, but I did not want to leave my husband or our children, and especially not our beautiful grandchildren.

The date of surgery was scheduled two days after the results were given. To me it was a miracle that I was able to accomplish so much in such a short time. Again, God intervened to have one person to cancel so that I could be added to the schedule for surgery that quickly. This, again, proved to me that *God was in every step of the way!*

After a biopsy was accomplished on these four sentinel nodes that were removed at the time of the first surgery, it was concluded that there was a sizable tumor in the first sentinel node, so back to surgery eleven days after the first surgical procedure.

Because of this lymph node tumor, the doctors recommended four chemotherapy treatments. I did not want to go through chemotherapy since my dad had died with the effects of his first chemotherapy treatment many years before. His blood dropped drastically, and it never returned to its original state. Death issued several months after that incident.

When the first part of December arrived that year, I was healed enough from my two surgeries that I could attend a play practice. I had planned to go that night when an icy rainstorm set in later that afternoon. George forbade me to go for fear that I would get sick and not be able to fulfill my acting obsession. I, finally, was able to attend my first play practice, the practice before the dress rehearsal. I was told where to stand and how to move on stage. I had already memorized my part completely. The dress rehearsal went without a hitch, and so did the performance. Thank you, Lord. The church was extremely gracious to wait on me for this performance. Thank you, Lord!

Since I first realized that chemotherapy would be needed, my first prayer was *"God, please shut the door* if this is not Your will for me to proceed ahead with these treatments!" I had a friend in Atlanta who was sending me many books about how other people had cured their cancer by taking natural products. This was intriguing to me, but the books I read proved that the person was able to make up his own treatment, and not even one book told details on what they did. Those books were not much of a help; in fact, they discouraged me from thinking "out of the box."

My prayer continued: "Lord, please shut the door if you want me to change my approach for the treatment!" My husband and I kept praying that particular prayer many times *every day*. At first, there was not a specific answer from God. Because I did not get specific direction for many weeks, I had my first chemotherapy four days before Christmas. I had various side effects due to that treatment and was in severe pain all over my body. Every bone in my entire body gave me great pain. My weight dropped drastically during this time period due to the horrible sores in my mouth as well as my intestinal tract, and every single hair in my head looked as though it had been burnt by fire. In a very short time, all of my hair fell out. This was very distressing! I was not looking forward to the next round of treatment; in fact, I dreaded it greatly! "Oh, God, please don't make me endure another treatment!" was my prayer.

It came time for the second treatment, and my prayer was still "God, shut the door if You want me to stop these treatments!" It was the middle of January 2011 when the next treatment was scheduled to take place. The Sunday night before my appointment, we experienced a very heavy accumulation of snow at our house. The office of the oncologist called on Monday evening to confirm the appointment via a computer call for the coming Wednesday, and I confirmed the appointment, much to my dismay.

On the day of my appointment, I was very concerned with the status of the roads. Our driveway and our road leading to the main road were windy with many areas where the edge dropped off into a deep ravine. I was nervous about sliding off the road into one of those areas. Our son came to help us properly apply the snow chains so that we could get down our hill/driveway and out to the paved road. When we arrived at the main road, the snowplows had already cleared the road. Praise God! We were then able to depart safely for the hour and a half ride to Gainesville for my appointment.

When we arrived, I stepped into the elevator and pressed the button for the third floor. The elevator did not seem to be working because it refused to close the door and ascend. When that elevator appeared to be faulty, my husband demanded that we should walk to our destination. We trudged forward up those three flights of stairs. I pulled on the door to open it, but it was *locked!* A thought flew through my mind, *This door is closed for you!* Wow! What a thought! Never have I ever had a thought such as that before or after that. God literally answered my prayer in what I thought was *just the nick of time!* To Him, He was exactly on time.

I will have to admit I then became *very angry* with the doctor and his office staff for not contacting me that they would not be available that day. I was furious! My doctor's office did not try to contact me at all that day to cancel the appointment that *they* had confirmed. Even when we checked our recorded messages that night, they had *not* left a message.

We then checked with the other offices in the same building to ask them to call my doctor's office to see if they were there. Two separate offices called, only to discover they were *not* there! Every doctor was in their office *except* my doctor! I even told my husband, "I am going to call them the next morning, and I will drive myself to get a treatment even if they will refuse to give me an appointment!" I felt as though they owed me an apology. A three-hour round-trip is a long way only to find that they were not there.

At that moment, I did not understand completely that God was shutting the door for the last time forever. As the rest of the day unfolded, I began to see that I would never again have to bear the horrible effects of my first treatment. I became very elated over that possibility.

My mixed emotions continued while driving home that after-noon. I was very distressed one minute and happy the next minute. It was hard to describe the emotional "roller coaster" that I was experiencing. At the same time, I was rejoicing that God had showed me His will in this matter. Still thinking that I would have to continue the treatments, I was nervous. It was a very unnerving day, not knowing what would be next. If God *shut the door*, what other adventure did He have in mind?

When we returned home that evening, we stopped at our mailbox on our road. I glanced at the mail to see if anything interesting was there. Then God revealed the next step of my adventure. Praise His name! Oh, blessed day! God clearly revealed the beginning of an adventure that was extremely exciting.

As I gazed on a book called *How to Cure Almost Any Kind of Cancer at Home* for $5.15/day by Bill Henderson, I was intrigued by it. As I glanced through it, my husband fixed supper, and I began to read it. Many times, I stopped to report the details to him. Finally, he said, "Just read me the book!" So I finished reading the entire book to him verbally, word-for-word. Not only, did it give many wonderful testimonies of people who had success in treating their cancer naturally, but it told of what products to use and where to obtain them. The next morning, I began to gather needed information from each company and commenced ordering from them. This is when I totally realized that God wanted me to experience the door being locked and no one at the office because it caused me to realize that God answers prayers specifically! I had told Him, "Please shut the door!" So He did just that! If the office had contacted me, I would not have seen that God takes us literally with our comments from our mouth or our prayers. I praise Him for being specific with His answer.

I have been engaged in this program for almost seven years, and I feel wonderful! Furthermore, the cancer has not recurred. I return to my surgeon every year for a checkup and have not had any difficulty thus far. Thank You, Lord!

A vast segment of my cancer treatment centers on the consistent use of *Essiac Tea*. This tea was formulated by the Indians from herbs found in the woods. Renee Caisse, a home health nurse in Canada, made her rounds as a nurse to many Indian homes, and they disclosed to her which herbs and how much to administer.

One day, she was assigned a new patient who was an elderly woman being treated for stomach cancer, and many doctors had done all that they could for her. Her primary doctor gave her two weeks to live because there was no recourse left. Renee asked the doctor if she could give *Essiac Tea* as a treatment for her. The doctor replied Yes! She was dying anyway! She started the tea immediately, and this woman died twenty years later due to old age.

I started using the tea in the early months of 2011, and I am faithfully taking it every day, 365 days yearly. It is a body detoxifier, and it removes all the impurities that we receive from processed foods, air, water with additives, and all sorts of environmental impurities. I feel great! This is something that I have committed to continue for the rest of my life.

Also, Mr. Henderson's book influenced me to study about a German doctor, Johanna Budwig. She was a medical doctor who practiced medicine in the early until middle 1900s. There is a clinic in Germany that still carries on her treatments. She also had a PhD in what I call "oil-ology."

She knew exactly what effect a variety of oils would produce to cure cancer in the human body. It was said of her that she would treat stage 4 cancer patients with a 90 percent cure rate for them.

I also follow other methods on how to beat cancer naturally, such as monitoring the PH of my body and eating foods that cause my body to become alkalized. Cancer cannot thrive in an alkalized body. If your PH is between 7.4–7.6 on the PH scale, this is a cancer-killing range. When someone first has cancer, this means that their PH is about 5.5, which shows that their body was extremely acidic at the time of cancer.

I am at present six and one-half years beyond my cancer. I am continuing my diet, *Essiac Tea*, the flax oil shake with fruit, vitamins and minerals, and monitoring my body's PH every day. I have resolved not to stop the entire program until the day God calls me home.

During this time, God has manifested Himself to me in so many ways. His presence and His hand has been felt every day. There is always a purpose for these trials that He allows us to face. They are not in vain. Sometimes God calls people home to be with Him, but I want to investigate for a moment how God moves during these trials.

I want to give God all the glory for my healing and saving my life. It all came from Him alone! To God be the glory!

The Bible states in 1 Peter 1:6–7 that God allows trials of all sorts in our lives to test "the genuineness of our faith."

> Though now for a little while, if need be, you have been grieved by various trials, that the genuineness of your faith, being much more precious than gold that perishes, though it be tested by fire, may be found to praise, honor, and glory at the revelation of Jesus Christ.

Also, God uses trials for judgment when we are in our sins, but that is not how God was expressing Himself in my life at that time.

This life in general is a "school of faith" through which God is putting all of us in order to manifest to each of us the reality of each person's faith in Him. If we get upset with God during trials and no longer follow His ways, our faith does not have the aspects of total dependence on Him that will withstand God's "refining fire." In 1 Corinthians 3:5–16, this reveals what are the needed aspects of "true faith" in God. These passages show us that we have to build our life on only one foundation—Jesus Christ (v. 11).

God is real; He is listening; He loves us; He has paid for our sins at an infinite price. Jesus is looking for a personal love from you and me. He also expects an obedient commitment on our part. Our reward will be eternal life both now and forever. John 17:3 sums up what eternal life is: "And this is eternal life, that they may know You, the only true, God and Jesus Christ whom You have sent."

What reality does your faith have—that of trusting self or doctors only, or is it that of fully trusting in God alone for healing or deliverance? Doctors are great. And they do a mighty work in helping us to heal. But God is the One who gives them the wisdom and causes them to be creative in developing various cures for diseases. It all starts and ends with God!

God means for His children to *rejoice* that the Lord is King; Your Lord and King adore!

Rejoice, give thanks, and sing, and triumph evermore. Lift up your heart, lift up your voice! *Rejoice*, again I say, *rejoice!* (Charles

Wesley). A rejoicing heart is a gift from God! In James 1:2, God tells us to "count it all joy when you fall into various trials, knowing that the testing of your faith produces patience. But let patience have her perfect work, that you may be perfect and complete lacking nothing." Furthermore, in 1 Thessalonians 5:16–18, we read, "*Rejoice* evermore, *pray* without ceasing, *in everything give thanks;* for this is the will of God in Christ Jesus concerning you."

Romans 5:3-5 speaks of a similar concept as James,

> And not only so, but we glory in tribulations also; knowing that tribulation works perseverance (patience); and perseverance, character (experience); and character, hope. Now hope does not disappoint, because the love of God has been poured out in our hearts by the Holy Spirit who was given to us.

What we have seen so far is that Christians are to *rejoice* in everything, *pray* without ceasing, and *count it all joy* when various trials come our way. These are commands from God!

I say these things to let everyone know that we had many opportunities in 2010 for *rejoicing,* for *praying,* and *counting it all joy.*

Barbara Johnson, in her book *So, Stick a Geranium in Your Hat & be Happy!* says, "Pain is inevitable but Misery is Optional." We all will experience pain and suffering throughout our entire life. We will experience trials of various degrees, but what we allow this pain to produce in us is totally up to us. Will we feel sorry for ourselves and live in the depths of despair? Or will we rejoice in the midst of the pain and sorrow and allow Jesus to give us a rejoicing spirit in this life? The choice is up to you!

2

Love At First Sight

Now that you have been introduced to me, I need to start back earlier in my life when I was still single. I want you to get a picture of who we were and what we had in mind for life.

This was now January, 1966. After Christmas 1965, my cousin and I journeyed to her house in Wilmington, Delaware for a fun week before I entered the University of Georgia as a junior.

Since I had been with my cousin for the last week in Wilmington, Delaware, I took a very slow train from there to Athens, Georgia, where my parents met me. I believe that it stopped in every single small town between Wilmington and Athens. That was the longest train ride that I had every taken!

I believe that the main reason it was so very long was that I did not have a bed where I could sleep. The conductor came to tell me that there was a bed available, but I turned it down for fear that I would not get off at the correct stop if I went to sleep. He assured me that I would, but I refused to change my seat. I slept very little that night as the train was jostling me about with constant stopping and starting. I was exhausted by the time I arrived at Athens.

It was morning leading up to noon when I entered my dorm assignment. My biggest problem was that I had not eaten since I left my cousin. Since it was a sixteen-hour trip by train because of stopping at every small town, I was starved.

I thought that my parents would take me out to eat since it was noon the next day, but they had eaten before they picked me up. I never told them that I was hungry because I was so excited to be there starting the next chapter of my life at the University of Georgia.

After arriving at the university in the first few days of January, I entered the school of education with a major in speech therapy. This was a brand-new major that had recently been offered. I loved it.

Where I was slated to stay at first was the basement of Mary Lyndon Hall, adjacent to Snelling Hall cafeteria. It was completely filled with bunk beds, and there must have been one hundred girls who were to sleep down there. It was rumored that those girls were to remain there until a room became available in another dorm.

As I was bringing my luggage down the hall heading to the basement, I met an old friend, Vickie, and we had quite a reunion. Vickie and I had graduated from Savannah High School together in 1963. She and I both were very excited to see each other since we had not seen each other since we graduated. I told her what I was doing, and she immediately said that there was an empty bed in her room that would house three girls total. Her room even had a bath connected to it, which was unusual. It was a large room that had three study desks, one bunk bed, a single bed, and plenty of extra walking space, plus it was on the first floor.

She immediately went to the housemother and asked if she could have her friend take that empty bed. I was elated at the possibility that I would not have to sleep and try to study with those girls in the basement. The basement was literally wall-to-wall beds with very little walking space. I never could imagine how they were going to study in that situation.

The housemother said, "Yes, you may have your friend in your room." Praise God from whom all blessings flow! So instead of having to figure out where I would study, or how I would be able to sleep with noisy roommates, or who would get the shower next, I settled into a very spacious room with adjoining bath with only two other girls. God, you are so very good!

As soon as I settled into my new room, my parents left to return to Savannah, which was a six-hour drive. Daddy had to go back to work the next day.

I enjoyed my new major very much and studied hard for the first four months. I was even nominated for "Who's Who in American Colleges." To me, this was an honor in itself. By the first part of May, I was feeling like I would like to meet a nice young man whom I could date.

I had one class with a friend from Savannah High who was a boy. We never dated, but we were friends. I asked him one day if he knew any really nice guys at the University of Georgia. He thought for a moment and said, "Yes, in fact he is from Savannah as well!"

"Wow!" I thought. "How perfect!"

My friend explained to me that he would be at Snelling Hall cafeteria at the cash register at the right aisle at five minutes to seven that evening. He also explained that he would be the only one manning that serving line at that time. It was five minutes before closing, so he said that he would have time to talk with me.

"Oh, wow! I was ecstatic!" I went to my dorm room, took a bath, fixed my hair, and found the outfit that I thought was my best color. And then I waited for that time to arrive.

Just before that time, I proceeded to walk to the cafeteria. My heart was beating fast, and the closer I came to it, the faster I walked. *Would I meet my prince charming? or would I be disappointed? God, will he even look at me? or would he be too busy and not notice?* I mused.

I appeared at the door to that line exactly on time. Of course, I was the only one present since it was time to close. Everyone had already finished eating and had gone.

I looked down the line to the cash register before I found that guy. *There he was standing by the register.* I looked at him, and he blinked both eyes at me. I looked away because I did not know what blinking both eyes meant. I thought maybe he had an eye problem, so I decided to take a second look. This time, the same scenario happened.

I gazed at him again, and he repeated this gesture. I again looked away and thought, "Oh, well! What did that mean? Does he have an eye problem?" I'm glad that I did not realize that he was winking because the Bible tells that we should beware of men who wink (Proverbs 6:12–14, 10:10). But, of course, he was not a perverse man or a fool. He was only a young man who liked what he saw coming in the door.

By this time, he had come to the head of the line and was asking me what I wanted to eat. I showed him, and he checked me out. I waltzed over to a seat, and before I knew it, he was over there sitting with me. He was very nice and cordial. We chatted the entire time that I was eating. I found out that I knew his sister from high school and that he lived on Talahi Island, which is right outside of Savannah going toward Tybee Island, which is Savannah Beach. I knew exactly where that was because my boyfriend from high school lived only two houses down from him.

That was the most exciting dinner I had ever had. Before it was over, he had my phone number. He called me that night, and he asked me to go to a dance with him that Friday night. Since this was Tuesday, I had to wait a few days, but that was fine because I had to study for a major test coming up that Saturday at noon.

Friday night arrived, and my *prince charming* arrived with his rather old *yellow chariot*, which actually was a 1957 station wagon.

The dance was so much fun! I enjoyed every moment with him, and I could tell that he seemed to like me. By this time, I was floating on top of the world!

Before he left to go home that evening, he asked me to go play tennis and to eat breakfast the next morning before my test at noon. I agreed.

The tennis match was exciting as we both kept hitting balls over the fence. We were forever having to retrieve them before we could continue. It really was not playing tennis as neither of us were accomplished tennis players. It was only hitting the ball back and forth on the court; that is, if we could hit it. Nevertheless, it was the most fun

I had in quite a while. It did not matter what we were doing, but that we were together having fun!

Since we were not truly playing tennis, we decided to eat breakfast. That was the best part of that morning. We chatted and continued to get to know one another.

When we returned to my dorm, I would be preparing to leave for a week off since it was Mother's Day weekend. But first, he wanted to talk outside the dorm. He kept making these kinds of statements "When we get married . . . !" I was so upset by those statements that I finally ran into my dorm. As I was leaving, I yelled, "See you when I get back!"

There were several of those statements, and they scared me to death because we had only met on the Tuesday before, and now this was Saturday. Somehow, I had to concentrate on my test, and it was hard to pay attention after someone had spoken those words to me.

I went home to Savannah to spend the week before I was to return. My family and I had already decided that we would spend that next week at my uncle's house. My cousin, Beth, was only two years younger than me, and we would share our heart with each other, especially about our boyfriends.

That night, I explained to her the activities of that week and what he said on Saturday morning. She suggested that we pray and ask for God's will to be done in this matter. We both prayed and went to sleep.

The next morning, she said, "How do you feel about our prayers last night?" I replied, "I feel as though I should return and get to know him better before I stop dating him." Even though he was moving too quickly for me, I was enjoying him and all the attention he was showing me.

"Was God the one who was bringing us together? Would I be missing the delight of my whole life if I refused to go out with him?" I thought.

I did not want to let him go, but at the same time, I did not desire to stay with someone who may not be faithful to me. I was not sure about him only because I really did not know him yet.

I returned to the university, and we dated over the next two months. By this time, it was the middle of July. He again started talking about getting married. That was good then because I had already decided that this was God's will for me. Actually, he never officially asked me to marry him; his way was to say "when we get married." So he never proposed to me ever even to this day!

We both agreed that we would ask my parents if we could marry in August. When we asked them, my mother was very upset since we had not known each other very long. My dad was not pleased either about August since we hardly knew each other for only three months. They were both afraid that I would not continue in college, and their desire was for me to complete my college.

My dad related to us that day that he would be in favor of us getting married in December, but not August. However, my mother was exceedingly upset with him for making this known.

We were thrilled at this possibility! As the next month proceeded, we began making plans for a December wedding. As we prayed, the Lord seemed to be opening some doors for a December wedding. We were encouraged!

I wanted to marry on December 18, which was a Sunday afternoon. As I went to reserve the church, I found out that my cousin's friend had already reserved it for that day at four o'clock. I was disappointed as we wanted to marry the week before Christmas and then enjoy Christmas with my family.

I proposed to my mother that we marry during that week at night. She was very ugly to me that our guest would have to wear long dresses, and that was terrible to her. I assured her that I would make it very clear that they could wear their regular dresses and not evening wear. She flat-out said no!

We had no recourse but to marry on Christmas Eve that year, or else we would not have been able to marry for another year as I had to go to summer school to complete a five-year program in four years. So at four o'clock on that Christmas Eve, we were scheduled to marry. She was not pleased, but we had Daddy's blessing. From the time in May that we met to the day we married, it was seven and one half months. I can understand why my mother was upset. But we felt as though it was the best thing to do.

God orders man's steps in Psalm 37:23 "for the steps of a good man are ordered by the Lord, and He delights in his way." We knew in our heart that this was the right thing to do for us. It seemed to be impossible to wait another year when our hormones were running freely. We knew that it was time for us to marry and not to wait.

God works through circumstances of life to direct His children's path. We knew that "God had done great things for us; we are glad" (Psalm 126:3).

Thank you, God, that Your Almighty hand was so evident and timely in our meeting each other. Thank you, God, that you answered my prayer so promptly.

3

Covenant Readiness

The fall of 1966 was filled with preparations for the wedding. Oh, the day for which I had always waited, even from childhood, was now approaching rapidly. Every bride I ever saw was an inspiration to me. I believe that I wanted a dress like each of them.

Even while in high school, I wondered what kind of dress would I choose when my wedding day finally came. I often tried out each boy's last name whom I ever dated to see if I liked the sound of it. But of course, not one ever popped that question.

In fact, all that George ever said to me before we married was "When we get married . . . " and fill in the blank. He has never to this day ever proposed to me. He never, never ever asked "Marywinn, will you marry me?" or any other variety of that statement. He assumed from the first date that we would someday marry. I suppose that it was love at first sight!

The wedding date was the first problem that needed to be solved. As I told you in the last story, Mama was not a "happy camper" about a December wedding. She wanted it to be the next summer, but that was not a possibility, as I needed to be in summer school in order to graduate that next June a year later. The earliest we would be able to marry would have been Christmas one year later or two summers later. I thought, "What an awful thought for a young couple!" That would be more that our hormones could handle.

As I mentioned in my last story, my cousin's friend was getting married on that date that we originally chose. Mom absolutely refused for us to get married during the week at night. So the only date available was Christmas Eve, December 24, 1966.

After we nailed down the wedding date, I needed to purchase a dress. All my life, I had dreamed of having a lacey dress. I dreamed about the design and how gorgeous one made of lace would be.

Since my mother was unquestionably angry with me about the wedding date, she refused to think about going shopping with me to pick out a dress. I went once by myself. I tried on many dresses that were lacey, but they actually looked horrible on me.

I felt so alone when Mom did not want to cooperate with us. I did not go anywhere else shopping for a dress. At this time, we visited an older couple who helped George as a teenager. She volunteered to make my dress. Since Mom was not being reasonable, I agreed, and we were about to proceed with buying the material needed. When I told my mother of her offer, she said "No!"

Just a few days later, Mom came to me and related that the Lady Jane Shop in midtown Savannah was sponsoring a bridal fashion show that featured all the latest styles of wedding dresses. We both attended together. It seemed as though that she decided as my mother, that she should help me instead of my older friend. I think she was jealous!

There must have been thirty or more different styles, fabrics, and colors to choose from. The champagne color for a wedding dress was being introduced that night. The fashion design for the most elegant dress of the evening included frilly lace and was of a champagne color, not white.

Mother immediately fell in love with that one. But the one that I liked best of all in those thirty was called the "budget dress."

All Mom could talk about that night going home was the dress that was the highlight of the evening. I was not thrilled with it because I had tried on frilly and lacey dresses that did not do anything to make me look wonderful.

The budget dress had an A-line skirt that was simply beautiful. Also, I did not want to choose an expensive one so as not to give Mom another reason to be upset.

The Lady Jane Shop announced that they would be open at nine o'clock the next morning if you wanted to be the first to try on the spectacular one. The clerk was convinced that I had come early in order to be the first in line for the champagne dress.

When I divulged my choice of dress, both my mother and the clerk were disappointed. I did not consider the champagne dress because of its color and its frilliness. White was the color I wanted and nothing lacey! Another reason I did not like it was because it was sleeveless for a December wedding.

As soon as I had seen the budget dress the night before, it appeared to me to be just exactly what I wanted. I was first surprised when I saw it with its simple beauty. When I tried it on, I knew for sure that this was my dress! To me, it looked as if it was tailor-made just for me!

I was not excited about the veil that they had chosen to be worn with it. I suggested that I should get a long veil much like the one that my mother had for her wedding. She promptly obtained a *Bride's Magazine* for that month so that I could pick out which veil I wanted. She assured me that any one of those designs could be ordered and received in plenty of time for the December wedding.

When I tried on the budget dress with the veil in *Bride's Magazine*, it was an exquisite combination. To me, it was perfect! The veil gave the dress an accent that it needed. It dressed it, and it was the perfect accent to compliment this dress' simple beauty!

My mom must have talked to my dad about thinking that this dress was not pretty. He came to me and told me that I could choose any one I wanted regardless of the price. But I explained to him that I did not choose the budget dress because it was cheaper, but because it was simply beautiful!

The next order on the agenda after choosing my dress was to pick out the bride's maid dresses. I found exactly what I wanted at the Lady Jane Shop. The top of the dress was a deep Christmas green in color with beautiful roses embroidered in the sateen material. The bottom of the empire waistline was a light-green crepe material that flowed just down above the floor. The dress had a dark green sateen bow that trailed from the waistline to the bottom of the long skirt. It also was simply beautiful!

All of the bridesmaids were kin to me. My maid of honor was my cousin Dorothy, who was involved in the "almost wreck" when I was nineteen. My cousin Suzanne, who came home from camp to have lung surgery, also sang at our wedding. My other cousin Beth was another bridesmaid along with George's sister, Marti. The junior bridesmaid was another cousin, Cathy, and the junior groomsman was Keith, son of George's friend as a teenager.

As time marched on and December came, the florist wanted to know what color green to make the ribbon for the bridesmaids' flowers. I related to them that Christmas green would match the bridesmaids' dresses.

The flowers were being grown by my uncle who specialized in camellias. I requested that he pick red or the variegated red-and-white in order to bring out the Christmas colors. He so graciously agreed to supply all the flowers necessary for the entire bridesmaids' party.

The weather in Savannah prior to December 24 was so very pleasant and especially nice for securing these flowers. At night, the temperature would drop in the high forties, but in the day, it would be pleasantly warm with possibly a light nip in the air as afternoon closed in, leading to evening.

As it drew closer and closer to our appointed date, my mother secured an appointment with her hairdresser on Friday, December 23. This appointment was made for my cousin, Dorothy, Mama, and myself to have our hair washed and designed for the wedding.

My cousin arrived the day before our hair appointment. She shared with my mother and me the hair spray that she was in the process of developing at her work. She had brought some with her that she wanted us to try at our hair appointment the next day. My mother was leery of using something brand-new that had not been fully tested and placed on the market yet. But Dorothy and I both encouraged her to let us try it.

The hour came, and off to the hairdresser we proceeded. It was a joyous occasion for me to know that this would be the last time before I was married when I would be having my hair styled.

As the beautician completed our styling, she proceeded to reach for her hair spray. My cousin spoke up and loudly proclaimed, "No! Use my hair spray."

My mother expressed her concern about this, but Dorothy and I encouraged her once again.

The beautician so sweetly complied to our wishes. So home we went to get ready for the rehearsal dinner. It was held at my uncle's house just following the rehearsal at the church. The meal was especially delicious as my aunt was an exceptionally good cook.

"Wow! The hour is approaching rapidly for my wedding," I thought. This made me contemplate the seriousness of this covenant on which I was about to embark. As every young woman draws nigh to the hour that she and her lover will be exchanging vows, it should be a very sober time. This is the hour in which she no longer is an individual choosing her way for herself, but she now is a young woman giving herself to her lover for the rest of her life.

In our day and time, this thought is foreign to the minds of young people in the world. Many are giving themselves to each other long before marriage or even in the place of marriage.

The Bible speaks of one man and one woman making a covenant together forever! It starts in Genesis 2:24, which is immediately after the first woman, Eve, was made from Adam's rib. It states, "Therefore, shall a man leave his father and mother, and shall be joined unto his wife, and they will become one flesh."

Men and women in marriage have a unique relationship together that should never be broken! We are "one flesh"! Not two separate individuals desiring to try to make it in life together, but "one flesh." "One flesh" cannot successfully be separated without the death of one of them or both.

More importantly, marriage is not a contract but a covenant relationship! There is a huge difference between these two:

1.   A contract can be broken by one or both parties.

2.   In marriage, a covenant is an agreement between two par-
     ties. The two parties are not the two people, but God and
     the man and woman. You say that is three parties. No, it is
     not! The man and the woman will become one party at the
     wedding. So it is between the "one flesh" and God!

When you consider that when you marry, the two individuals
become one together in marriage in Genesis 2:24. So this covenant
is a special relationship between one flesh (the two individuals) and
God. This can never be broken in God's eyes.

In Matthew 19:3–9, Jesus was asked a question by the Pharisees,

> Is it lawful for a man to put away his wife for any cause?
> Have you not read, that He who made them male and
> female said, for this cause shall a man leave his father and
> mother, and shall cleave to his wife: and they two shall
> be one flesh? Wherefore, they are no more two, but one
> flesh? What, therefore, God has joined together, let not
> man put asunder.

The Pharisees carried this conversation into another question.

> Why did Moses then command to give a writing of
> divorcement, and to put her away?" He said unto them,
> because of the hardness of your hearts, Moses allowed
> you to put away your wives: but from the beginning it
> was not so. And I say to you, whosoever, shall put away
> his wife, except for fornication, commits adultery: and
> whoso marries her which is put away commits adultery.

My point today is not to show when you could get a divorce,
but to point out that God never, never intended that any two people
divorce.

In other words, this is a serious matter, and it does not need to
be taken lightly. Consider carefully before you get married or before
you give yourself to someone and not seal it with marriage. God
hates both states!

Marriage is the foundation of a nation and God's church. A nation that has rampant divorce rate is a nation that will fall. God's church is crumbling because of the divorce rate being so very high also.

Make wise decisions by studying and examining God's Word on this subject. He has much to say about marriage and its permanency.

4

A Preparation for Life

God will reveal Himself in people's lives in various ways. He may give you a *rhema* from His Word tailor made specifically for you, or He may bring words to your mouth that begin to speak forth before you even have a chance to think, etc. Both of these illustrations have happened many times during my life.

I consider one instance that words spoke forth out of my mouth that were not prepared in my mind before they leaped out. This particular occasion happened three days before our wedding day.

It seemed like a normal day of preparation for the most exciting ceremony that I have ever experienced. It was December 21, 1966. My mom was giving me the last party before the wedding where our close friends and family were invited to come view all the wonderful gifts that we had received. Also, this was the last time as a single woman that I would have time to spend with my friends.

This was a *drop-in* party that was taking place all afternoon. We had not only a constant flow of guests, but the house was filled with many different people all afternoon. When some would leave, others flowed in. It was very enjoyable.

It was getting later in the afternoon when a very special guest stepped into our house. Her name was Gracie Butler. At this point in her life, she was in her early nineties. She was a contemporary of my Grandma Winn. She was spry and full of life. But most of all, she was filled with the Lord's Spirit. She portrayed love, joy, peace, long-suffering, goodness, faith, meekness (power under control along with kindness), etc. (Galatians 5:22).

By this time, the house was filled with friends, mainly older, from our church. This guest was a true Bible scholar of her time. She had been taught the Word of God from a child, plus she had studied it in depth for herself. Scriptures flowed from her lips without having to prepare.

Many people that day were astounded by her knowledge including me. As we stood around talking with each other, she added her views on many subjects that were being discussed. It did not matter what the subject was at that moment, she had a Scriptural answer from God's Word. She was a sweet woman that would graciously speak the words of life into people.

When she left this party, the women of the church were standing around in one circle by this time. They were praising her by commenting on her depth of wisdom that was pouring forth from her. In my mind, she was the *most-godly* woman that I have ever known.

As the women were admiring and commending her for her godly wisdom, my mother spoke up. She said "Oh, how I wish that I knew the Bible the way Gracie does!" Without thinking, out of my mouth flowed these words, "One day *I will* know the Bible the way Gracie does!"

I was actually shocked at these words. No one realized that I was speaking words that, I believe, God placed in my mouth. I knew that I had not prepared in my mind to speak them. That instance made such an impression on me as a young woman, in fact more than I realized for many years to come. Now I truly believe that those words changed the entire course of my life.

From that moment, God began in me a journey of life that has never stopped. Within the first five years of that time, God had caused both George and me to change our spiritual focus to His

Word. He gave both of us a desire to know His Word, and He gave us a desire to learn the Word by ourselves as well as through other's teaching.

He placed us into a group of young couples that were truly seeking God in a special way. This group was led by an older, more mature couple. This was the beginning of God speaking to us through His Word. God taught us through this group to understand how to study, meditate, and memorize His precious Word. Even though we did not have total Biblical understanding, He began to *fan the flames* of desire in our heart to know and teach His Word (Matthew 12:20; compare Isaiah 42:3). God fanned these flames even though they were very small. Through the years, we have truly grown in grace and the knowledge of our Lord Jesus Christ (2 Peter 3:18).

This one statement I made has been the secret root of glorifying God. Because I was willing to be taught and led by God, He has brought much fruit into my life and our life together (John 15).

I am positive that Gracie influenced so very many people in the course of her long life. In fact, my dad came to know Jesus because of Gracie's teaching in the adult Sunday School class at our church.

The power of Gracie's testimony in my life lives on long after her death. I believe that God is extending Gracie's fruit after her life through her planting a desire for God's Word in me. If it was not for her and her testimony for the Lord, I would not have wanted to seek God and His Word all of my adult life. She spurred in me a desire to know God in a way that changed the course of my life. This is the one event that has led me to seek God with all my heart. Thank you, Gracie, for being true to God for your entire life.

All of us, whether young or old, are being watched by someone younger than ourselves. We have a potential of giving a witness in a positive way in someone's life. I believe that when we get to heaven, God will reveal how we made a difference in other's lives. Will our influence be positive or negative for God's glory?

Gracie showed me how to abide in Jesus (John 15:4–5,7–10,16). In the Scofield Reference Bible, Mr. Scofield defines abiding in Christ. He remarks "some people feel that Christ was referring to the power that He would grant to those who would remain *in Christ.*

According to this view, the meaning of the phrase is seen in verses seven and nine. Christ desired that His disciples continue to obey the words that He had spoken to them so that their lives would be full of joy.

Another view continues the meaning of this phrase. Showing that it reflects one's dependence on Christ, communion with Him, and obedience to Him. Remaining in these things will result in one's life becoming fruitful for Christ. For the believer, Christ alone can provide the grace and provision of needs in life. Thus, he must remain faithful to his service for the Lord and to the study of the scriptures in order to bear fruit".

I believe that all of these points can be pressed into one meaning for abiding. The first view shows *the power* that we will have if we remain close to Jesus. "If you abide in Me, and My words abide in you, you shall ask what you will, and it will be done unto you" (v.7; compare 1 John 2:19). Again, in verse nine, "As the Father has loved Me so have I loved you: *continue you in My love*". We will have the power of the Holy Spirit if we continue in God's Word and His love. Truth of His Word should never be spoken apart from the love of Christ.

The second view reflects our *dependence, intimacy*, and our *obedience* to Christ. These three things must be in our lives in order to be fruitful. We cannot have one foot in the world and one in the church. That does not equal abiding. Both feet must be solidly founded in the Word of God and obedience to it.

True power of the Holy Spirit is not in emotionalism. You will be emotional when the Holy Spirit takes control in your life, but it does not stop there. How can you have God's Spirit moving in your heart without getting emotional?

At the same time, our emotionalism has to be founded in knowing and obeying the Word of God. Through this, we will be emotional when we consider how great a God we have by looking into His Word.

The results of abiding in God's Word hinges on our obedience to Him. Through obedience, we will have the power and love of Christ flowing through us to others.

The power of God flooding our heart will result in fruit. First, the fruit of ridding our life from known sin. We need to allow God to make us a "new creature in Christ" (2 Corinthians 5:17). We need to live a godly life apart from the *world*.

After becoming that new creature, God has given us the ministry of reconciliation" (2 Cor. 5:18). Reconciliation is all about proclaiming the death, burial, and resurrection of Jesus to the world of unbelievers. In other words, how are you going to proclaim the truth of God's Word to others?

If the power of God is truly flowing in and through us, we will have a strong desire to proclaim Christ to a dying world. We will be wanting to find new ways of telling others of God's love. If you are not concerned with witnessing to others, you had better ask God to examine your salvation to see if it is true (2 Corinthians 13:5).

Gracie never missed an opportunity to graciously proclaim the truth of God's Word. Her name was Grace and truly she portrayed the power of God while at the same time revealing His truth. She lovingly salted each word with the grace of God while speaking His Word in His love and justice. Praise God for saints like Gracie.

5

Wedding Bells Pealing

Today is the day that I will give myself to George forever! It was a beautiful December day as the sun was shining and the warmth of the morning was blossoming. It was unusually warm for this time of year. I arose from my sleep and peered into the mirror.

"Oh no! What happened!" I screamed as I viewed myself. My hair was hanging limp and appearing to be extremely oily. "I can't get married looking like this!" I screamed.

As my mother and cousin all came running to see what the screaming was about, they were horrified at my countenance! Dorothy began to say, "I believe that I had better revise the formula for that hair spray.

My mother kept shouting, "I told you not to do it!"

Yes, somehow mothers always know best! I had to agree with her on this subject.

She quickly called her hairdresser, who graciously offered to redo my hair before the wedding. Since the wedding was not until four o'clock in the afternoon, we had plenty of time. I drove myself to the beauty parlor since Mama and Dorothy thought that they could do something with their hair. As I was returning to my car, the air felt as though there was a *bone chilling breeze* that had not been there all week. A blustery gust of breeze began to blow as if a north-eastern wind was setting in for a storm. "Oh *no!* Did my uncle pick my flowers yet?"

It was not yet noon, but the air felt as though it were the middle of a winter night. The gusts of air were particularly chilling almost to the point of freezing. When I returned home, Mother called to make sure that all the flowers were safely inside. My aunt related that uncle was picking them as they spoke.

"Will Uncle Wally manage to save them before the winter breeze taints them with brown?" I considered. "Oh, well, there isn't anything that I can do!" I contemplated. God will have to protect them and give us beautiful flowers.

Just before Mom, Dad, Dorothy, and myself left the house for the church, my mama came into my bathroom as I was applying my makeup. She began a conversation that I was not sure where it would lead. The statement that hurt me the most was, "If this does not work out, you cannot come home!" I was stunned! I could not believe that she was saying these things. Of course, in my mind, it was going to work out. We loved each other, and neither of us had the thought of leaving each other.

I could not believe that she was making this statement just moments before I was to leave for the church to dress for the happiest day of my life. I was shocked and hurt by her statement. I told her that this is going to work, and I would not want to come back!

George and I both had the intention that it would work out from the beginning. We never doubted that. Divorce was never a possibility! Staying together for the rest of our lives was our only thought.

Onward to the church, I went, trying not to allow that statement to negatively color my day. As we arrived, my thoughts went immediately back to the happiest day of my life—the day that I will give myself wholeheartedly to George forever!

Mother helped me dress, and pictures with my family were in full swing. We proceeded down the corridor to the foyer of the sanctuary when I caught a glimpse of the bridesmaids' bouquets. "What army-green ribbon!" I exclaimed. That florist had put army-green ribbon with the red camellias instead of Christmas-green ribbon. Army-green looked rather sick next to the Christmas-green in the dress. "Oh well, what could we do? Nothing. By this time, that was the way it was!" I told myself.

So down the aisle, the bridesmaids proceeded one by one. When I realized that this was the very minute that I had longed for most of my life, I took a deep breath hoping to relax, but instead, I could not catch my breath. Nervousness hit me like a ton of bricks!

My dad patted my hand and quietly tried to calm my spirit. I took one look at George, and there was no way that I was going to calm myself. Immediately, tears of joy began to seep out of my eyes. I did not wipe them away—they just rolled down my cheeks onto Daddy's coat sleeve and onto his hand. I was smiling as big as I possibly could. In fact, after a few minutes, I thought that my face would break if I smiled anymore. I am not able to express the pure joy and contentment I was feeling inside at seeing *my prince charming* and *my knight in shining armor* waiting for me!

This was the ceremony that led up to two becoming one flesh. That was a powerful thought at how God miraculously makes two separate people one flesh (Genesis 2:24). From now on, we would function as one and not as two people. The man, being the head as Adam was created first, and Eve was created from man's rib, meaning that she would be under his authority. This is God's order for harmony—provided that neither will take advantage of the other.

As I kept on proceeding down the aisle, I felt as though I was *Maria* in the *Sound of Music*. My veil was as long as hers, and my dress was as simple and beautiful as hers. My bouquet was as grand and pompous as my mother's bouquet had been thirty-two years before when Mom and Dad married.

As the whole wedding party gathered across the altar, ready to commence the remainder of the ceremony, I gazed at my beloved's face, and again tears welled up in my eyes. As we said our *I dos*, I felt as though I could hardly speak, but I sweetly whispered my loving answer to my beloved.

As my cousin Suzanne began to sing the Lord's Prayer, the pastor, George, and myself made a tower of hands as we all knelt at the altar. You will never believe what happened next!

I realized at that moment that my tears that I had been weeping while going down the aisle and I seeing my beloved's face did not just disappear, but they were collecting in my sinuses. As I bent my head to pray, I felt like a long silvery cord hung under my nose. I opened my eyes to see it proceed up and down as I tried to sniff it back up into my nose. When I inhaled, it shrunk closer to my nose, but it never went back into my sinuses. As I took another breath, it elongated as a silvery spider's web hanging from my nostril. It was going up and down as I breathed or as I sniffed. Because we all had our hands in a tower on top of each other, I was not able to retrieve either hand from the pile, as the men were pressing down on them heavily.

George finally realized my dilemma and jerked his hand free of this tower, reached in his pocket, and pulled out a handkerchief, and he wiped my nose for me. Praise God for an attentive husband!

His first duty as my husband was to wipe the snot hanging from his beloved's nose during the most important ceremony of our lives. I was thankful because what would I have done if I had to walk down the aisle out of the church with snot dancing in the breeze as I walked? I had no hands with which to wipe because one was holding my bouquet as I walked out, and the other was holding my lover's arm.

As we were walking back around to commence taking pictures, I heard a voice calling, "Mrs. Lent!" I turned immediately, even though it was a strange last name to me at that point. It was my stepmother-in-law greeting me for the very first time with my brand-new last name. I was proud to be Mrs. Lent now!

Right before we married, my aunt had teased me about my whole name. Now it would be Marywinn Rentz Lent. What a mouthful! Try to say that fast. It is a tongue twister.

When I think back over the engagement and the wedding ceremony, I am struck with the fact that faith in God and faith in George came hand-in-hand into this commitment from the beginning until the end.

First, I had to have faith in God that He was leading me to the one whom He had picked for me. Then also I had to have faith that George would do what he was promising as a fiancée. "Would God let us down and not fulfill His promises in His Word? Of course, not!" His Word is "yea and Amen!" (2 Corinthians 1:20–22).

Now that I look back after fifty years, I had no assurance that George would do what he promised. I can understand the cautions that my mother had for us. I felt them for our children as they were getting married, but I will say this: I never said to any of our children that they could not come back if it did not work out. Never! I knew that they would work it out when hard times would come. For come they would!

As I take Jesus by faith in His Word, so I had to, so to speak, take George at his word. I realize that this comparison is faulty because Jesus is God and George is not, but it still stands because if I do not have faith in my-to-be husband, I should not marry him. If he had given me any reason to doubt what he was saying, I should have broken the relationship off at that point.

Faith, trust, hope, love, and believing in each other have to be interrelated in a marriage.

1.   The foundation of marriage has to be Jesus Christ as God. Both man and woman have to give themselves separately to Jesus as their Savior and Boss of their lives before they come together in marriage. That is foundational to any marriage. If it is not based on this foundation, it will crack and crumble when the storms of life arise. And arise they will!

2.   As I have to trust in God with all my heart (Matthew 22:37–39, Mark 12:28–34), so I needed to trust in George also with all my heart. I must love God supremely, and my love for George would come next. I had to realize that God and George had my best interest in mind from start to finish.

3.   Hope in God is not a *maybe* but a solid truth that will happen in time to come. As we hope that one day we will spend eternity with God on the new earth, so I had to hope in George as my protector here on this earth today.

As we have hope in Jesus, our hope is based on the His resurrection from the dead! In 1 Peter 1:3–5, we have a living hope, not a dead hope. If Jesus were still in that grave, we would have a dead hope. Praise God, He is not dead but was resurrected from the dead and is seated at the right hand of the Father right at this moment (Matthew 26:64; Acts 2:33–35, 5:31, 7:55–56; Romans 8:34; Ephesians 1:20; Colossians 3:1; Hebrews 1:3; 1 Peter 3:22).

As sure as Jesus was resurrected from the dead in the power of the Almighty God, so we will also be resurrected in the last day as true believers (1 Corinthians 15:3–4, 12–28). This is an inheritance that is "incorruptible, undefiled, and that does not fade away, reserved in heaven for us who are kept by the power of God" (1 Peter 1:4–5).

The power for our marriage has to be in God alone. We do not have the power to sustain a marriage forever. Only belief in God could do that!

1. Love for God had to come first before my love for George. We should love God supremely and also, next love each other (1 John 4:11). My love for God should issue into a love for George only above all others (Exodus 20:14 compare with Matthew 5:27–28).

2. Believing in Jesus is a must for salvation, just as believing in my husband is a must for a solid marriage. Without believing solidly in Jesus, we have no salvation, for Jesus is *the* way, *the* truth, and *the* life, and no man comes to the Father but through Jesus (John 14:6).

So believing in my husband that he will be true to me is a must. If you have any doubts as to the sincerity of your mate's love, break it off until you can be sure of his fidelity.

Be sure in your heart that God has led both of you together forever!

Here is Marywinn with her three bridesmaids, junior bridesmaid, and my cousin, Suzanne, who sang at the wedding.

6

Our Celebration Was Exciting!

This is a picture with the candle that burned my
veil while we were feeding each other cake.

As we completed our pictures, our celebration with our friends and family was exciting! My whole family was in attendance at our wedding and celebration, and also George's family except his oldest sister. She was not able to attend.

Even though we were married on Christmas Eve at four o'clock, our friends and family were so gracious to take time away from their own family to celebrate with us.

The reception started immediately after the ceremony because standing on the sidewalk outside of the reception hall would have frozen our guest. Remember how I spoke of the weather changing from spring-like to a winter storm condition in a matter of minutes at noontime? Because of that, we opened the hall for guests to visit with each other as they waited for us to complete the pictures.

As we came into the hall, all clapped and greeted us cheerfully. We began to mingle and talk with our guests as we were excited that all had come on such a special day.

After many pictures with various guests and our wedding party, as well as servers at the reception, we commenced to cut the cake.

As we both were having fun trying to stuff the cake into each other's mouth, my uncle ran up to me and started beating on my head over my veil. As I was completely surprised by his action, I screamed, "What are you doing?"

He quickly explained, "As George was trying to stuff cake into your mouth, your veil touched the flame of the candle. Quickly, a hole was burning in your veil, and the flame was moving fast in this material. So before this hole could burn farther, I jumped up and put the fire out." Thank you, Uncle Herman!

That hole is still in my beautiful veil to this day. I am thankful to him for being observant to what was happening because I wasn't!

As the hour was growing late, I retired to my dressing room where I changed from my wedding dress to my beautiful cranberry-colored winter suit with a dark mink collar and a cute mink hat to match. And, of course, I want to point out my brown alligator shoes and pocket-book. I was fit to kill in my up-to-date outfit!

The next exciting thing that would happen was on our way to our honeymoon. My brother, during the reception, was busily preparing our car for the trip. First, he wrote all over the car "Just Married!" Of which, I was glad he did because I had dreamed as a child of having a car decorated with "Just Married" and cans flowing from the back of the car to the ground in order to cause a lot of noise. Naturally, this would bring lots of attention to us as we traveled. That was very exciting to me!

Also, my brother somehow was able to get our car unlocked to fix up the inside also. And as we ran through loads of people to the car, we both jumped in the driver's side on a busy street. "Thank God, no cars were coming!" I thought. We sped off leaving our family and guests in the dust. No one followed. I was glad of that.

The first thing that we did was to turn on the heater to get warm that night. An awful smell began to permeate the air. "Yuck! What kind of smell is that!" I shouted.

Soon George figured out that my brother must have placed "sardines" in our heater. After we drove to my parent's house a short distance away, I went in to pick up our electric blanket. George took the heater apart and retrieved the half-cooked sardines that my brother had so carefully placed there just for us.

Also at my parent's house while I was inside, George washed the "Just Married" signs off our car. I was highly disgusted with him because I had dreamed as a child to drive through the city with our car highly decorated with those signs. I was upset with him to no end! "But, George, I loved those signs!" I shouted. Oh, well, gone forever! Likewise, he took the cans from behind the car. What a boring ride we then had! This was our first argument as a married couple.

But at least we were off on our honeymoon. My mother had encouraged us to go to Florida for a winter honeymoon, but wanting to think for ourselves, we refused. A friend from college told us about her area. It included Callaway Gardens at Pine, Mountain Georgia. She had made it sound grand and glorious. However, in the winter, the gardens were not in bloom. We had only some flowers in a hothouse to look at. They were beautiful but did not keep us busy for a week.

Our first stop on our travels on Christmas Eve was to rest that night in the bridal suite at Holiday Inn in Statesboro, Georgia. It was great! Of course, George carried me over the threshold of our room. The room was especially beautiful and comfortable as we had a king-size bed and other amenities.

The most exciting part of our honeymoon was the second night. We traveled on Christmas day to our final destination at Pine Mountain. We had a reservation at a cabin in F. D. Roosevelt State Park.

Because we were traveling on Christmas Day, no gas stations were open for very long that day. We had a terrible time finding even one gas station open, or even one restaurant. We arrived at the Ranger's house late that afternoon. By this time, the ranger was not eager to show us to our cabin as he and his family were still enjoying their Christmas party. We felt bad about interrupting him, but we had no idea which cabin was ours.

It sounded exciting in the winter to honeymoon in a cabin in the woods with a fireplace, a kitchen, one bedroom, and a bath. It sounded like a snuggly, quiet, out-of-the-way, secluded spot for a honeymoon couple.

When the ranger came to the door, he admitted that he had forgotten to check the gas tank at our cabin to make sure that we had enough gas for heat and the gas logs for the fireplace. He reported that he would not be able to have the gas delivered until Monday and that he would not have it cleaned until then also.

We were both disappointed as we had nowhere to stay that night. I begged George to travel about twenty miles into Columbus, Georgia, to book a motel room for the night, but he refused. He took the ranger's suggestion of going to a cabin that had a fireplace with wood to heat in it for the night. This cabin was down in a hole below the road. It was one large room that housed a fireplace, kitchen area, a bed, and one bath was in a small room off the larger room.

The problem with it was that some of the cement that used to seal the wooden logs together had broken off, which created a hole in the wall. After researching this cabin, there were many places that had lost cement; hence, many holes in the wall.

The leaves from the outside of the cabin blew through these holes in the wall and covered the bed and floor. I was not excited because it was not clean at all. Also, the bed slumped down in the middle. As we lay on it, both of us went straight to the middle and rested at a standstill against each other with leaves in between. Undeniably, to George that was great! But I did not like falling in a ditch next to each other to sleep that night. Again, I was in tears, and we did not agree!

I was not a happy camper, and that was an understatement! That was the second time that I was greatly displeased with my new husband. I went back into the car and sat as we discussed what to do.

George, being a romantic, envisioned us cooking our steaks that we had brought with us over the fire in this cabin and then retiring to bed to snuggle to keep ourselves warm. He thought that it would be absolutely dreamy!

What could I say or do with a starry-eyed husband who thought he had it all figured out? He even suggested that he cook me the meal. So I had no choice but to concede as he suggested.

The meal of steaks over the fire was wonderfully delicious along with a salad and a baked potato. By this time, the cabin had warmed slightly, but the wind still wiped through the holes in the cement.

After supper we were desiring to retire in bed. Being a passionate young adult, he demanded that I put on one of my fluffy, lacy nightgowns instead of my immensely warm one. I complied, and we went to sleep.

During the night, the fire subsided, and the weather outside was frightfully cold; hence, a cold wife. I tried to snuggle to him, but that was not sufficient for the low temperature outside.

The next morning, I was able to talk him into going over to a cabin at Pine Mountain. This cabin was very sufficient. We had all the amenities for eating, sleeping, and bathing along with a large living area. It was extremely comfortable. We had a wonderful heating system there.

We enjoyed a bicycle built for two the next morning after we relocated. The bike paths were great as we drove from one hothouse to the other enjoying the flowers. It was a wonderful day, as we were able to get some exercise and enjoy the cool refreshing winter air. It invigorated us to want to go back to the cabin and enjoy a gas log fireplace while sipping a hot cup of chocolate.

As the next day dawned, I woke up feeling dizzy. Also, one of my ears was hurting. I rested as he cooked breakfast. After that, I was beginning to feel better, and I was able again to go bike riding to enjoy the mountain views. The mountains at that time were a wonderfully different view from the seacoast and the city of Savannah.

We spent two more days enjoying the mountains by trails to waterfalls and much more. The mountains were breathtakingly beautiful.

We came back on that Friday instead of staying until Saturday because my ear had worsened and my dizziness was back. I called my mother and asked if she would call the doctor and get me an appointment that day. She did, and I was able to get medicine to start feeling better.

We enjoyed the mountains immensely, but I believe a trip to the mountains should have waited for the spring and summer. All I have to say is that I should have listened to my mom about going to warm Florida instead of to the mountains.

All in all, it was a wonderfully exciting wedding and honeymoon. I still look back on it with humor and contentment. I don't believe that I would have traded any part of it for anything.

My comment to others who are contemplating a honeymoon is to take into consideration what knowledge older adults are trying to impart to younger people. They have been around the block more times than we have been. They do have wisdom that young people have not yet experienced.

They are not just trying to control us but are trying to make life more pleasant than it would be if you do what your selfish self wanted. Open your heart, listen, and drink in the wisdom that they have for you.

God gave us older, wiser people in our life to guide and direct if we would but listen to them. Parents may sometimes act as though they are trying to control our lives, but really, they are trying to impart much needed wisdom from their lives to our life.

Wisdom is one of God's attributes. He is "immortal, invisible, God only wise" (1 Timothy 1:17; Jude 25; Romans 16:27). In Ezra 7:25, God reveals that He imparts wisdom from Himself to people on this earth.

When I was a young person, I felt as though I knew as much as any adult, but of course, this is false thinking. God has prepared the older people with trials and hardships that make them wise and alert to dangers that young people have never experienced.

Now that I am old and had experienced myself many hardships, I want to agree with David, the psalmist, in Psalm 71:18–19: "Now also when I am old and gray-headed, O God, do not forsake me until I declare Your strength to this generation, your power to everyone who is to come. Also, Your righteousness, O God, is very high, you who have done great things; O God, who is like You?"

God has placed in me as an older adult a strong desire to tell the next generation what He has done for me so as to influence them to keep seeking Him no matter what comes their way. Even in the midst of the severest trials, God is in control. This is one of the primary reasons for sharing my book: to proclaim the mighty acts of God in our life so that others will be encouraged.

I was young once, and now I am old and now I desire whole-heartedly that I speak into the lives of younger adults. I remember how I felt and what I thought as a younger adult, so I want to help others through the trials of life.

I ask, if you are young person, please allow older people to speak into your life. They will give you wisdom from experience that God may use to redirect your life.

Here is an analogy in our life that young people need to consider. If you think of an archer with a bow and arrow, think of the older people in your life as the bow. The younger adults are the arrows that the bow will shoot forth into this wicked and perverse world to win souls for the Lord or to redirect lives for His glory before it is too late. Remember, you are an older person to someone, so redirect a younger person's life no matter what age you are. You are older than that younger person.

Be willing to listen to wiser adults. I encourage you to give them entrance into your life, for they have much to say. You will have to give them entrance, for they cannot push their way into your life without your permission. Even seek an older couple to adopt you, spiritually speaking, so that they can share some of the pitfalls of their life before you fall prey to them. Be wise and listen!

Here we are heading off for our honeymoon with my cranberry colored suit, with mink collar and hat accented with my alligator pocketbook and shoes.

7

The Coast Calls Us

George graduated in June 1967 with a doctorate in veterinary medicine, and I graduated June 1968 with a bachelor of science in education with a major in speech pathology both from the University of Georgia. Upon graduation, George was praying about what God wanted him to do next.

Already Dr. Mood, the veterinarian from Savannah, Georgia, who helped him when he was a teenager wanted George to come to work for him in Savannah after he graduated. It was a comforting thought that he already had a job as soon as he graduated.

So George began working in Savannah immediately; he noticed within a few days that the wife of the veterinarian was instructing him on how to treat the animals. Within five months of the time he had initiated this new relationship, George knew that his time there was limited. In November of that year, he investigated the possibility of changing jobs to Atlanta.

I had just completed the fall quarter at Armstrong State College in Savannah where I was able to take certain courses that would transfer to the university for my graduation soon. Next, I returned to University of Georgia in order to complete my last two quarters when George secured a new job in Atlanta. His start date was January 1, 1968. I was more than excited to hear that. I did not want to be in Athens completely away from my husband.

George located a job in Chamblee, which is part of the Atlanta complex. Dr. Greenway was getting older and was looking for a younger veterinarian to possibly take over his practice.

George said good-bye to the Mood's, and we packed up to travel to Atlanta. In fact, they loaned us their horse trailer to move.

George commenced his work in the new veterinary clinic in Atlanta and was excited that he decided to leave Savannah. It was easy for me to go back and forth on the weekends to Atlanta, or for George to sometime come on Tuesday evening and spend Wednesday with me at school. Wednesday was my light day for classes.

During the spring quarter, I was a student teacher in the DeKalb County Public Schools. I had a great mentor teacher. She was in her thirties and had taught for many years.

At the same time, George was praying about what to do next with his veterinary work. Atlanta was nice for those six months, but we both knew that neither one of us wanted to stay there.

Dr. Greenway and his wife were very gracious to us and took us under their wings to help us. We were very dissatisfied in our church situation, and they took us to their Baptist church. We enjoyed it greatly. That is when we switched denominations and became Baptist.

In those six months in Atlanta, George was praying fervently about what God had for us next. By this time, he knew in his heart that he wanted to have a veterinary clinic of his own and not work for someone else.

He began to buy veterinary equipment to furnish his own clinic. We were on a shoestring budget as we did not want to overextend ourselves with a loan. Our aim was to save what we could to buy and then wait until we had more money to purchase more.

He also realized that he did not want to buy an existing clinic either. Our finances would not permit that. Slowly but surely, as we had extra money, he purchased various supplies that would be essential in a veterinary practice.

These many months of functioning in two separate veterinary practices had given him vital information on how he would choose to establish his own veterinary practice. So he began to seek the Lord for His will in our lives.

The next question was where would this veterinary practice be? We talked with my family about a place that did not have a veterinarian yet. I even considered Darien, Georgia, as that is where my family had a cabin on the inter-coastal waterway that I loved very much. That is where I would have wanted to go, but at that time, the town was extremely small, with no potential for a thriving veterinary practice. We called our property Harbor Hill, and that is where all my best childhood memories are.

But a member of my family suggested Hilton Head Island, South Carolina. This was a new, thriving young community that was beginning to burst at the seams and did not have a veterinarian yet. George was enthralled with the idea, and I loved the fact that it was close to my family.

In March, we went down there to visit and investigate the possibilities. George first went in to Sea Pines real estate office to inquire about placing a veterinary clinic on the south end of Hilton Head. Sea Pines was the most developed community on the island at that time, so he conversed with them about the possibility of having a veterinary clinic on some of their land.

They were interested at the idea, but they immediately said that they had restrictions about what we could or could not do. They offered to build a building to house it, but the calenture for us was that they could tell us what we could and could not do. This was a negative thought for George.

We scouted around again on the north end of the island where Port Royal Plantation was in its infancy stage. We visited Mr. Fred Hack Sr. to ask if he knew a great location for a veterinary clinic.

He sent us to the industrial park area to visit Mr. Joe Pitts Sr. We found Mr. Pitts in his office behind a garage apartment building. We discussed our thoughts with him, and he was excited about hearing this proposition.

That day, he offered us the possibility of renovating the garage apartment in the front building into a veterinary clinic. He also suggested that we live upstairs.

This was the most exciting news that we had all day. He seemed to be very accommodating to our wishes. Later, he shared with us that he and his wife had a son and daughter-in-law who were about our age. If they had needed help, he would have wanted someone to help them, so that made him want to help us. Thank God for moving Mr. Pitt's heart to help us with this provision.

This was a prime section of the island to have a business, as there were already many businesses located there. The electric company for the island was positioned next door to this property. We agreed to rent this building and property that day. Both parties were excited about this endeavor. It almost seemed too fabulous to be true. But true it was!

Mr. Pitts was extremely helpful and encouraging that day. We went back with the idea that this is where we would begin our endeavor. He gave us a reasonable price for renting this building. He agreed to remodel this building to make it ready for occupancy.

We returned to Atlanta for the next several months to make ready the contents of this practice. Every day that George was off from his veterinary commitments, he was gathering equipment for the bare necessities of this new business.

When the spring quarter at the University of Georgia ended for me, I graduated June 1968. We packed Dr. Mood's horse trailer with our belongings, and off we departed for Hilton Head.

George was driving his 1957 yellow station wagon while pulling the horse trailer that housed our furniture and veterinary equipment. I was driving my blue-and-white 1966 Chevrolet car that my parents had bought for me the first spring at the University of Georgia right before I met George.

George was having a rather unpleasant trip that day in his old car with no air-conditioning. It was the middle of June, and he had our several cats inside this car with him, along with most of our clothes and kitchen items.

By the time the car started moving, the cats started yowling as only cats can do. This was a piercing sound to human ears, so shortly after the car started moving, the cats were removed from their box so that George would have peace and quiet. This meant that the windows had to be rolled up so that the cats would not jump out. Can you imagine driving for six hours with the windows rolled up with no air-conditioning in an old car in hot weather? George experienced this for the next six hours.

My car was cool and comfortable. But it was packed to the hilt with our clothes and other small belongings. Off we went on our new endeavor. We were both very excited!

Neither of us were afraid of the coming months. We both were confident that this would be a success. We both understood the potential for a growing business and no debt associated with it at present.

We arrived at Hilton Head, and a young man met us there named Darrell. At the time, he was living in the building adjoining

Mr. Pitt's office, which was in the back. He unlocked the apartment and clinic and helped us move our belongings into both places.

The biggest difficulty was that the apartment did not have a stove in it. But that did not disturb us because we had a grill with which to cook. We placed the grill on the screened-in porch upstairs in the apartment, and we were in the business of cooking.

The weather was hot, but not unbearable. Usually, there was a great breeze that was sweeping across the back screened porch. The apartment did not have air-conditioning at this time. We had a fan that moved the air around enough at night so that we were able to sleep comfortably.

The first morning, we had put many boxes on the ground outside the veterinary clinic. We were sorting each drug and piece of equipment to discover the best placement for each.

As we were busily working on this, we had a car pull up, and the people got out to talk. They had a dog with them that needed our services. So we treated our very first patient on the grass outside that day after we arrived. George began ravaging through the drugs for the correct ones.

We talked with these people for a long time as they were interested in hearing our story as to how we chose Hilton Head. They greeted us joyfully and made us feel welcomed. They turned out to be extremely good clients for many years. They were an elderly couple who passed away within the first ten years. But up to that point, we took care of all their animals. It was encouraging to have the first patient so quickly.

The word of the veterinary clinic spread rapidly to the uttermost parts of the island. We immediately were working, and we never had slow time for the first many years. The most of our clients on the island were wealthy people with many animals.

That day at Hilton Head, we could see the hand of God moving in negative and positive ways to unlock His will for us even though we knew almost nothing about the truth in His Word. In spite of our lack of knowledge of God's Word, He was still opening and closing doors for us. When God shuts a door, He opens a window of opportunity. He shut the door for the clinic being on the south end of the island but opened the window for the north end to house our clinic. God uses various circumstances of life to mold our ways. This day, we were very aware of His mighty helping hand.

In the Old Testament, God stretched out His miraculous hand and wrought wonders for the children of Israel against Egypt. God reveals in Exodus 7:4–5, "Pharaoh will not heed you, so that I may lay My Hand on Egypt and bring My armies and My people, the children of Israel, out of the land of Egypt by great judgments. And the Egyptians shall know that I Am the Lord, when I stretch out My hand on Egypt and bring out the children of Israel from among them."

Again, in Exodus 13:3, God reiterates, "Remember this day in which you went out of Egypt, out of the house of bondage; for by Strength of the Hand of the Lord brought you out of this place." Also in verse 9, God repeats, "For with a Strong Hand the Lord has brought you out of Egypt."

God gave the children of Israel the Passover in Exodus 12, and in Exodus 13:14, He instructed them that when their children, in time to come, would say, "What is this?" The parent and grandparents were to tell them, "By the strength of hand, the Lord brought us out of Egypt."

Furthermore, in Exodus 14:21, 27, God instructed Moses to stretch out his hand toward the sea.

> Moses stretched his hand over the sea; and the Lord caused the sea to go back by a strong wind all that night, and made the sea into dry land, and the waters were divided. So, the children of Israel went into the midst of the sea on dry ground, and the waters were a wall to them on the right and on the left. The Egyptians pursued and went after them into the midst of the sea, all Pharaoh's horses and chariots, and his horsemen . . . And Moses stretched out his hand over the sea . . . the sea returned to its full depth when the Egyptians were fleeing into it. So, the Lord overthrew the Egyptians in the midst of the sea.

Here we have the powerful account of the mighty, strong hand of God through Moses upholding His children. Since God upheld His children in Exodus, so He will uphold His children today, "for He is the same yesterday, today, and forever" (Hebrew 13:8). "I am the Lord, I do not change" (Malachi 3:6).

God miraculously closed the door at Sea Pines but opened a window with Mr. Pitts. Thank You, God! That certainly was a most sufficient supply for us. We did not need a grand and glorious clinic where we would be controlled, but God opened His provision through a simple circumstance that left us free financially to follow His ways.

Correspondingly, God also used an older man to guide us as a young couple into financial freedom and still acquire the needed business arrangement. Mr. Pitts, a simple but loving man, spoke into our lives in many ways in the future, which will be discussed later. Praise Your Name, O Lord!

We are enjoying life at the Hilton Head Island Veterinary Clinic.

8

The Need Is Not the Call

After George graduated from veterinary school and worked one year with two veterinarians, the Lord called us to the coast. We lived and worked in a renovated garage apartment building. Originally, in the downstairs veterinary clinic, we had one room for each of these areas—waiting, examination, surgery, and restroom. Off the surgery zone, there was a small area that led to the runs for the dogs to go outside. This facility was located on a half-acre of land.

The pens for boarding animals were through the back door, which led to the next building. George built many pens of all sizes for large and small dogs or cats.

The house was directly above the veterinary clinic. It had a living room, extremely small kitchen, two bedrooms, and a bath area. It was perfect for us since we did not have children. I helped George for the summer in his clinic, but in August, when school started, I had a job in the public schools in Hilton Head and Bluffton as a speech therapist. This was a brand-new concept to all the schools in this area.

All summer, I enjoyed cooking on our grill on our screened-in front porch. We also had a hot plate in the kitchen for pot cooking.

This served us well for those three months and also in early fall. The summer brought much business so that we began to have a surplus of funds. The Lord is so very good!

But our aim was not to be extravagant with our money. We were trying to conserve all that we could in our savings account as we desired to purchase our present location from Mr. Pitts.

Because of this, we went to buy a small apartment-sized stove in order to save money, and what's more, our kitchen was extremely small. We only had to turn around in one spot to touch everything in this kitchen. There was not enough space to accommodate a full-sized stove.

We went into Bluffton, a very small town close to Hilton Head, to a store that sold everything, and I mean everything! Many of the items had been repossessed from lack of payment by the first owner.

This was the case in our apartment-sized stove. The price was a whopping twenty-five dollars! It was in great condition. We loaded it on the back of my dad's truck and took it back to our house. Now I would not have to cook outside in the cold weather. Praise God!

That was our first big purchase after moving to Hilton Head. Shortly after this, Mr. Pitts offered us a great price for purchasing this entire property with a mammoth garage that had five bays that we would be able to rent. Additionally, it included the clinic below and above apartment building, and it also had another elongated building out back with Mr. Pitt's office attached. He had a water company business that was headquartered there, and he agreed to rent this from us if we purchased the entire property.

He helped us secure a loan from the Small Business Administration. We originally bought our half-acre with many buildings on the Industrial Park Boulevard for $21,000 to be paid off in seven years. Our payments were $320 monthly. What an opportunity the Lord gave to us! We entered Hilton Head when most of the plantations did not exist, or the market showed lower prices because they had not yet been completely developed at that point. There were two young and beginning-to-thrive plantations—Sea Pines and Port Royal.

Soon it was time for me to commence working as the very first speech therapist at Hilton Head Elementary School, Michael C. Riley High School in Bluffton, and Bluffton Elementary School. I traveled to each school weekly.

Michael C. Riley School was the most difficult of all my schools. All that I was trying to do with these high schoolers was to correct outstanding speech disorders so as to make life easier for each of them. They did not seem to understand what my purpose entailed.

Since I was the only white face in the entire group, they made life almost unbearable for me. I always arrived at noon when everyone was outside for lunch break. I had to try to make my way through the crowd in order to go to my speech room. They just stared at me as I tried to enter. They held their ground and would not move to allow me to pass. I was weaving my way through the maze of students in order to find a hole toward the door. No one was smiling back or helping me get in the door. In fact, they seemed to be occluding the door to prevent me from entering.

I tried to discuss this problem with the principal, but he would not meet with me. My supervisor finally released me from that school for lack of communication with anyone on that campus.

One of the major problems was that this was the first year ever for these schools to be introduced to speech therapy. Speech therapy was a brand-new major in colleges at that time, and public schools in this area had never dealt with this in the past.

Mr. Wilborn, the principal at Hilton Head Elementary School, was proud that the children spoke in the black dialect in their culture on the coast of South Carolina. He was concerned that I was coming in his school to teach them how to speak the way that I spoke. I spent some time discussing what my purpose was and that I was only looking for true speech impediments, not cultural dialects. He finally understood, and I was able to then function in this capacity as a speech therapist was expected to accomplish. I had a very good experience there that year, and we understood each other. He worked with me to help me accomplish my purposes.

At Bluffton Elementary School, I was accepted more there than I was at my other two schools. This was the only white school that was part of my agenda. However, the custodian at the school was the only person who ever gave me a hard time about trying to help his child overcome a lisp. He literally cussed me out and refused to sign the waver to allow me to work with his child.

Our first year on the island was a record year for how many new organizations popped up on the scene to want the young people to join and help their cause. The older citizens were introducing many new ideas that they wanted the younger citizen to do. After setting these up, the older people sat back and did nothing to help. These included the fire department, rescue squad, Rotary Club, and the Junior Chamber of Commerce. These were the four organizations that George belonged to and attended their meetings on a regular basis.

Fire department night was every Monday night, Rotary Club was every Thursday at lunch, rescue squad had many training sessions to learn how to properly handle different cases very often. Many Saturdays were spent learning the proper protocol for ambulance attendants; plus, there were weekly meetings to keep everyone in touch with the latest procedures.

Since we were both raised Methodist, we began to search out a Methodist Church on the island. Finding none, we realized that one would soon be established within one week. We went to its first meeting and became charter members of the very first Methodist Church on the island: St. Andrew's by the Sea.

George became lay leader by default. Since he was not at the meeting, he was elected, so they made him the official lay minister, and he did not refuse it. Also, he taught a children's Sunday school class for several years.

He was scheduled up with activities; there was not any time to spend with his wife. I felt as though I was a widow when I was not.

When I would be working all day in very difficult circumstances at school, I wanted to share with my husband the drama of the day; but instead, he was off at a meeting to help the community. What he was doing was not bad, but it did not help a young marriage.

I grew particularly tired of being left out quite a number of nights per week. George had a brainy idea that since we did not have any children yet, I should join the rescue squad. "You could be my partner on the ambulance," he said. That was not exactly what I had in mind, but I complied.

One night, we were called out to transport an elderly woman to the hospital in Savannah. I was driving, and he was in the back with the patient. The specific time of the night was midnight. It was in the fall of the year. There was a mist rising up from the marsh and river that night that was beginning to occlude the night air. The air was particularly frosty that evening.

As we drew closer to Savannah, we were passing across the road that was surrounded by marsh. The roadway was extremely difficult to see. A car began to hover particularly close to the back of the ambulance. I was going as fast as I could for conditions, and the emergency lights of the ambulance were flashing so that others were aware that we needed to proceed as fast as we could to the hospital.

The road was actually an elongated causeway through the marshlands that led to small rivers. This car was bothering me because he could not have gotten any closer. If I had stopped suddenly, he would have plowed right into the back of the ambulance. I devised a plan that would get him off my tail. I picked up our loud speaker and shouted, "Get off my tail!" He immediately dropped back, never to be seen again.

That person must have thought God was talking to him, for where else would a voice have come from in the middle of the night in *nowhere!*

It appeared that he joined himself to me so that I could blaze the trail for him to see where we both were going. We successfully maneuvered across the wide-open marsh to the Savannah River bridge and safely to the hospital. That was the last ambulance duty that I ever had. Shortly thereafter, I found out that I was pregnant.

Being service-minded toward others is a wonderful calling, but *the need is not the call.* There are tremendous needs all over this universe. There is not any way that one person by themselves, or even by uniting with others, could ever meet all of them. Jesus says, "Love they neighbor as thyself," but we must not attempt to do that with detriment to your own loved ones.

George's desire to help others did not last only for that one year. He was the volunteer fire chief for the next ten years, and he was a member of the Rotary Club the entire eighteen years we lived on Hilton Head. He was on the rescue squad for almost as long as he was a fire chief, and he was a member of the Junior Chamber of Commerce for the entire eighteen years.

As we began to have children, I was at home with babies all day and all night. Sometimes he would go from work directly to meetings without even coming home to eat supper. He ate late when he returned home.

The fire department was the one activity that brought the most danger. Sometimes, when I think back on those ten years as chief, I praise God that he is still alive. Fires are very hazardous, especially when he had to enter burning buildings in order to transport elderly or disabled people to safety.

One young man about our age was a member of the volunteer fire department on the south end of the island; he died due to injuries sustained at a training session. He was climbing up and down on the rope, learning how to grasp properly so as not to slide down without being in control of his status at all times. Something happened, and he slid the entire way down without control and landed on the pavement. Even though he had a hard firemen's hat on his head, when his hat hit the pavement, the helmet crushed his head, and he died.

There are many times George was in grave danger in fires. I will relate some of the exceptionally dangerous activities that George did get into with many calls. Even one of our firemen died at a fire at the airport. George was the first fireman to arrive apart from that fireman who worked at the airport. This young man was already dead when George arrived. When I think back on those years, I am amazed at the safety that God provided for him during those dangerous years. Praise Your name, Lord! These will be shared in the future.

Don't get caught in continuous service for service's sake. God must be calling you into the service that He chooses for you.

Jesus was compassionate, loving, kind, and always doing the Father's will. There is the key—doing the Father's will! True, we must be about our Father's business also, but even Jesus did not heal everyone or minister to all. He was one person who had the same limitations that we do. He would get tired and could only be in one place at one time.

In John 15:12, Jesus reminds us, "This is my commandment, that you love one another as I have loved you. Greater love has no one than this, than to lay down one's life for his friends." God calls us to look to the needs of others around us and to help others, not just our family. Jesus' whole life is a testimony for reaching out to others, and He always was in the will of the Father and under the Father's control.

On the other hand, we must fight against being selfish. Iniquity is selfishness. Jesus "was wounded for our transgressions, He was bruised for our iniquities" (Isaiah 53:5). This chapter in Isaiah explains how He suffered and died for all our sins.

Peter gives us an exhortation: "Be as He which has called you is holy, so be ye holy in all manner of life" (1 Peter 1:15). One aspect of "holiness" is not being selfish; therefore, holiness is others-centered! We all need to focus on others and not just to our family only. We all need to have a ministry in this world that meets the needs of others as Jesus did, but it can't be all-consuming to the point of leaving family out.

First, God means for us to love God supremely; then secondly comes family, and thirdly, others. If we are being like Jesus, we will include others. Being others-centered means that we are becoming more and more like Jesus.

At the same time, God calls every husband to love his wife as Christ loved the church. In Ephesians 5:22–23, God instructs both wives and husbands in the proper balance of serving and loving:

1. "Husbands, love your wives, just as Christ also loved the church and gave Himself for her" (v. 25). Husbands are to pay attention to their wives and meet her needs, especially when there are children involved, not just do what they want to do.

2. "So, husbands ought to love their own wives as their own bodies; he who loves his wife loves himself . . .

Nevertheless, let each one of you in particular so love his own wife as himself, and let the wife see that she respects her husband" (vv. 28, 33). This is as proper balance for both husband and wife.

3.   "Husbands, likewise, dwell with them with understanding, giving honor to the wife, as to the weaker vessel, and as being heirs together of the grace of life, that *your prayers be not hindered*" (1 Peter 3:7).

When husbands neglect their wives, it is to the detriment of their prayer life. Be careful to get a proper balance with these thoughts. Let the Lord be the one whom you look to for understanding of what each person's ministry should be. Don't try to do all things that you see!

Remember, the need is *not* the call!

The picture with this story is George with his fire truck the first few years of being the fire chief for the north end of the island.

9

Our First Child

After I had worked for one year in the public schools of Hilton Head and Bluffton the very first year that we moved to Hilton Head, I completed that very stormy year with the thought that I wanted to go home and start having children. I had no desire to continue working, especially in schools that rejected the whole concept of speech therapy education.

George was doing well in the veterinary clinic. By this time, he had hired a secretary, and he was thriving.

The first few attempts of having a child failed. Nothing was taking place. My hormones never seemed to be functioning properly, even from my teenage years.

Let me take a moment to explain that in my family, this was not unusual. My mom and dad had experienced great difficulty in having children. For the first seven and one-half years of marriage, they were not able to conceive at all.

Mom seemed to be plagued with the problem of no menstrual cycles for many months at a time. Sometimes there would be no cycles for a whole year. So they decided to obtain help from a doctor.

Mom had gone to her gynecologist for help. He had put her on a sheep's ovary extract back in later 1930s. This seemed to have no effect. She was teaching first grade since she graduated from college, so she continued that since no children were forthcoming.

Several years later in the latter part of the year of 1940, she realized that she was gaining weight for some unknown reason. She went to the doctor to find out that she was truly pregnant. Since she had not had a period for more than eight months, it was hard to tell exactly when the baby was due.

The doctor first calculated that it might be the end of June of 1941. As the months progressed, she actually delivered May 8, 1941 with a seven-pound, six-ounce baby boy. Mom and Dad were ecstatic at his birth! They both praised God alone for this mighty gift to them!

As time went on during World War II, there were many years of rationing and hard times. Dad did not go to the military because he was truly color-blind. Mother now stayed home with my brother, Don, who was actually a junior in my family.

Not quite four years later, she again returned to her doctor because she was mysteriously gaining weight. She told the doctor that it was a baby girl. His reply was, "No, Mary, you have a tumor!" He stuck by his diagnosis, but Mom did not believe that, so she stuck by her diagnosis—a baby girl.

In a few weeks, even the doctor realized that she was pregnant for the second time, even though she had not had any periods for many, many months. Several months later she delivered her baby girl one week over her due date on October 2, 1945, not quite four and one-half years later. They again rejoiced at another miracle.

Many others in our family at large did not have any children. Some ended their thirties with no children, then conceived in their forties, but was only able to have one child. So I am from a family that had tremendous trouble conceiving and bearing children.

So it was with me in my teen years; nothing was functioning correctly. Even into my twenties, I would not have any periods for six weeks or two months.

Another problem that I had was when it came time for us to marry, my doctor gave me birth control pills that were, theoretically, to help regulate me. Since I was on them while in college and our first year at Hilton Head, we decided that we would discontinue them as we desired children.

I was never regular after that. No pregnancies were forthcoming. I went back to not ovulating at all and having extremely long cycles. I went to my gynecologist for help. He gave me a medication that would help me ovulate. We were so very excited that now I would be able to conceive.

At the same time, my cousin Dorothy was having heart surgery as a young woman at the University of Virginia. Her mother was deceased by this time, and she was not married. I was the only one who was available in our family to go to be with her.

This surgery coincided with my time of trying to get pregnant. The doctor had instructed me to take my temperature every morning to track whether I was ovulating or not. According to this record, I was not ovulating.

Just prior to going to Virginia to be with my cousin during surgery, my doctor had given me medicine that would stimulate ovulation. As I was tracking again my progress of ovulation, I was in Virginia when it should have happened. I was upset. How can I get pregnant when I am not at home with my husband!

One thing that I had noticed is that, for many days, there was no ovulation because my temperature was not going up. As the days progressed with my cousin, the surgery was completed, and she was recovering well. The day came for me to go home before I ovulated that month. "Oh, for joy! I still have a chance at getting pregnant," I exclaimed to myself.

Home I went, still in time to possibly be able to conceive. The day after I returned was the day that my temperature showed that ovulation had taken place. Oh, *excited* was not the word! That was truly an understatement!

Six weeks passed, and I made an appointment with my gynecologist. He sent me to have a test to see if I was pregnant. "Yes! I was truly pregnant! Praise God from whom all blessings flow!" I screamed aloud.

When the next month rolled around for a revisit, I was disturbed when the doctor told me that I possibly did not get pregnant at the time that I had first said, but I did not let that bother me. I was looking forward to getting larger so that I looked like I was pregnant. Every day, I would check my weight to see if I was gaining weight. "No! No weight again today! Oh well." At least I was not getting too fat for this time in the pregnancy.

On the next month, I returned as usual. My doctor reported that he believed that something was wrong, for my uterus had not enlarged enough for the number of weeks that I was pregnant. Oh well! I suppose the doctor was correct about me not getting pregnant when I reported. But that thought kept nagging me that I had the documentation to prove when I ovulated. This was in the back of my mind, but I would not allow it to surface in my primary thoughts.

Now it came to my fourth month! Surely now I would begin to show, and all will be well. Right before I was to go back for my appointment, I started to spot. The spotting turned into bleeding, and we called the doctor. He told us to get to the hospital immediately. Now it was a full sixteen weeks of pregnancy.

When I entered the hospital, the doctor examined me to find out that I was hemorrhaging in my womb. I was devastated! I thought that I was over the time that most women would miscarry. I screamed out that I wanted to save my baby. The doctor told me that there was not any hope of saving this one. My heart screamed out in total despair at the possibility of never being able to have a normal, healthy child! *Oh, God, HELP!* my heart cried out.

The doctor waited for my cervix to open so that the fetus would easily pass through the opening. After about five hours, my cervix was just as hard as it was when I arrived. Since the bleeding was still progressing, and because the nurse had not heard from the doctor in several hours, my husband said that he had to go take care of the animals that we had failed to do when all this started in the middle of the night. He had many animals that were boarding with us that needed attention. They had not been able to go outside for more than twelve hours. He said that he would do them quickly and be back before the doctor was ready.

As soon as he got on the elevator to go downstairs, the nurse came to my room and reported that the doctor was ready to take me to surgery. I told her to stop my husband, but it was too late. He had already left the hospital. Now I had to face this alone, and I did not want to do this, but I knew that I had no choice.

After surgery, my husband was already back, so I did not miss him very much. The doctor reported to him that the baby's heart had never started to beat on its own at eighteen days. The cord was extremely long and only had a "pea-sized" protrusion at the end of it. The baby never did develop beyond those first seventeen days. That explains why my womb was not enlarging as it should have been.

After this episode, the doctor explained that I may have trouble carrying any other children because they had to force the cervix open in order to do the procedure. I'm glad that it did not dawn on me what might take place in the future when I was able to get pregnant again.

I cried much over the loss of our first child. My thoughts went directly to thinking, *I might have to face the possibility of never conceiving again, or if I did, would I be able to carry it to full term?* This was totally devastating to me, and I prayed much about this situation. We both wanted this child, and we together were overwhelmed at losing our first child.

But God! Yes, this was truly one of those *but God* circumstances! I knew that God is still on His throne, and He had everything under His domain. To this day, I still cry over the loss of our first child. Even writing this story was very hard, and my heart is still crying. This occurred in the first few days in January 1970. To this date, it has been more than forty-seven years ago from the time of losing this child.

Someone might argue that this was not a baby yet because it did not look like a baby. At the moment of conception, God breathed into this child, and he or she was made a living soul (cf. Genesis 2:7). This pea-sized protrusion, no matter what it looked like, was developed into a seventeen-day child. This is what everyone looks like when they are in this period of gestation.

We will see our child in heaven one day. We will see him or her as if he or she would be in their height of perfection. I look forward to this day very much!

After many years, I would pray, *God, was this child a boy or a girl?* God has put in my heart that it was a girl. I have named her Christiana Joy! I look forward to meeting and holding our sweet little Christiana when I reach heaven. I never held her in this life, for she never developed properly, but I know one thing for sure: she is safe in the arms of Jesus (Fanny Crosby).

She must have been so imperfect that her tiny little heart never started to beat, not even once. But she was and is alive and well with Jesus. She developed for only those seventeen days before God took her. But oh! One glorious day, we will see her again actually for the very first time, and it will be a mighty day of rejoicing! Thank you, God, for this wonderful gift that you gave to us in her! We praise Your wonderful and glorious name for her. Thank You, Lord!

My heart agrees with Job: "The Lord gives and the Lord has taken away; Blessed be the Name of the Lord!" (Job 1:21b).

10

Victory at Last

After my very first pregnancy had ended, my gynecologist told us that we should give my body three months to heal from the effects of that pregnancy and death of our very first child. This was the longest three months of my life. I felt as though it would never end.

According to my temperature chart, again, I was not ovulating at all. My heart sank in despair. "Would I need to again take this medicine and have another child not develop properly?" I thought.

My heart was so anxious about trying the medicine again. But George and I both felt as though that was the only possibility of ever having a child. We prayed much about whether this was God's will for us or not. We both agreed that we should do it because God is in control of what took place. He knows the best for us.

Together, our decision was to return to the doctor for another prescription. By this time, it was three months after the loss of our first child. To be exact, it was spring of 1970. Oh, my heart was experiencing fear at the thought of trying again for a child.

We both realized that if we had a chance at having a normal child, it would be when we were still young. We did not want to wait and miss our childbearing years so that we would be less likely to have a normal, healthy child later. As I discussed these thoughts with my doctor, he encouraged us to try again. So try again we did!

I was twenty-four years old in the spring of 1970, but when the child would be born, I would then be twenty-five. This should be a wonderful time of life to get started with children.

Since we had tried the very first month of this medicine to have a child, and it failed the first time, my thought was to wait until the second month so that the first month could prepare my body and bathe it in the proper hormones. I wanted one month for the hormones to cause me to function properly before trying for a pregnancy.

Therefore, the second month it was! As I checked my temperature again, the second month had ovulation at the correct time about the fourteenth day. That was encouraging as this was the first time that it ever occurred in the middle of the month. Last time, it was very late in that month.

After six weeks, I made an appointment with my doctor. Yes, I was again pregnant. Thank You, God!

My next hurdle that I felt as though I needed to cross before I could be sure that this one would be fine was the sixteenth-week. Since our first pregnancy had ended at this mark, I wanted to be sure that I would not do the same thing.

As the days seemed to pass very slowly, that day was approaching. My heart was nervous at this time. "Would this be a repeat of the first time or not?" I contemplated. But God assured us as He whispered to me in my heart that it would be fine. "Thank You, God!" I whispered back.

As we were settling in our bed that night, I was laying on my back. All of a sudden, something that was a hard lump passed up to the surface on my abdomen under the skin and moved quickly across. I screamed, "George, feel this!" As he felt the mass, it moved down again where no one could feel it anymore. It lasted several seconds only to be hidden again. I started crying, "Thank You, God, I know that my baby is safe and healthy."

As I counted the weeks on the calendar the next day, I realized that it was the exact day that I had lost our first baby when I felt our second baby moving in my womb. That was very special to me. I knew then that God had given us a normal, healthy baby from Him. "Praise your name! Your goodness overwhelms me!" I cried.

As I progressed in the next few months, my husband's sister was to be married on December 17, 1970. Since I was showing by that time, I was not going to be in the wedding, but that we would help with various tasks.

It came for the night of the rehearsal dinner. By the middle of December, I was almost six months pregnant. Praise God! Soon it would be long enough to say that if I had this child, it would live outside the womb. That was very important to me since a friend had just lost a baby at this same stage, and I looked forward to passing over that time.

Well, the night before the wedding was here. The rehearsal dinner was in full progress when my abdomen commenced to cramp. We were sitting enjoying our meal when I felt as though I was either having a spasm, or was it a contraction in my lower abdomen? I whispered to my husband, and he took me outside so that we could talk freely about it. We walked around, thinking that maybe I had been sitting too long, and I needed to move around. But it increased as I walked.

We decided that we should go home so that I could go to bed and relax. I did sleep well that night, and all cramps had subsided.

We were glad since it was the wedding day. Oh, what a beautiful wedding it was, and we were so very excited for his sister and her husband to start their lives together.

After Christmas, I realized that I had to take my days easier since there were times when I would cramp again. When I returned to my doctor, he was gravely concerned at what had been happening. It was only the first part of January, and our baby was not due until the end of March. By this time, I had completed six months of pregnancy. He explained to me what to do when I experienced these cramps again. He told me to go to bed and call him.

I began to have these cramps several times a week, and when I would lie down, they would decrease in intensity. As I reported more of these cramps, he suggested that I should come every two weeks for a checkup.

On my next appointment, he examined me and reported that I had dilated slightly. By this time, it was the middle of January. His recommendation was to stay close to home and not go grocery shopping. I was in and out of the bed.

The cramps increased, and he said that it would be a miracle if I saw him on my next visit. He was expecting me to have the baby before that visit. By this time, it was the first few days of February.

We prayed that the baby would not come for many days yet as it was way too early. The doctor reported that it could come by the next day, but the Lord was gracious and gave us another eleven days after that time. "Thank you, Lord!" My praise for God increased with every passing day that the baby was still in my womb.

When it got to be February 14, I said, "Lord, if it is going to come in the next few days, let it come today." I thought that Valentine's Day would be wonderful birthday even though I really had another six weeks.

My friend at church that day remarked how the baby had dropped. That afternoon my husband had a veterinary meeting in Statesboro, Georgia, and he wanted me to ride up there with him, but I felt bad, so I did not go. He drove me to my parent's house an hour away, and I stayed with them that afternoon. When he returned that evening, I remarked to my parents and my aunt with my husband sitting there, "I believe that if I went to the hospital, they would keep me." No one appeared to hear me. No one remarked at all. They just kept talking.

On the way home, I made that statement again. "If I stopped at the hospital, they would keep me." My husband laughed and drove on. No one was listening to me. I knew that my cramps had increased steadily during the course of the day and evening. But we drove an hour back home that night. I should have washed my hair when I arrived home, but I felt too bad to do that.

At four-thirty the next morning, I was awakened by my water breaking. I screamed, "George, call the doctor, my water has broken!" He sleepily inspected the bed and assured me that I was correct! After calling the doctor, he also called his sister because she wanted to be in the delivery room with me, as she was a nursing student. The doctor allowed that to happen.

We had to again drive another hour back to the hospital from home. As we arrived, my cramps had turned into major contractions. Water was pouring everywhere I went. I handed the nurse my card that told her all my information. Her reply was "Honey, you are not due yet!" I let her know that I was aware of that! "But my water had broken, and my pains were overtaking me!" She seemed to be a little dense.

Subsequently, she commenced to examine me and rapidly called the doctor. She realized that there was not a doubt as to whether I was in labor or not. She prepared me for the delivery as well as preparing for the doctor's arrival.

George's sister had asked if she might be allowed to be in the delivery room with me as she was in nursing school. She was allowed to do that. By this time, Marti had taken her place in the delivery room over in the corner. I was in constant contractions. The only reason that I did not have it at home was because my bladder was severely distended with urine. This had kept the baby in the womb so that we could arrive at the hospital instead of having it in the car. Praise You, Lord!

As they relieved the overextended bladder of urine, the baby proceeded forth. The doctor attempted to relieve the pain by doing a spinal injection, but the baby proceeded out immediately after turning me over on my back. This injection did not have time to take effect. As I screamed, the nurse gave me gas for the actual delivery.

In a few moments, the doctor called to me to look at our beautiful baby boy! I picked up my head, and the doctor shouted, "Don't pick up your head because we gave you a spinal!" It was too late by this time.

The baby was so very perfect and large for this stage of gestation. It was so wonderful to gaze my eyes for the very first time on our beautiful, healthy, perfect little bundle from heaven. I wanted to hold him and love him, but the nurse took him away to the nursery. The doctor assured me that the nurse knew what she was doing, and it would be best for him.

In Psalm 127:3–5, God reveals His love for children, "Behold, children are a gift of the Lord, the fruit of the womb is a reward. Like arrows in the hand of a warrior; so are the children of one's youth. How blessed is the man whose quiver is full of them . . . " (NASB). Your Word, oh God, is so very true!

Our little George Edward was born on February 15 at six thirty in the morning. He was fashioned by God so very flawlessly. From Psalm 139:13–16, we understand that God formed his inward-parts; You wove him in my womb, and he was wonderfully made . . . his frame was not hidden from you when he was made in secret and skillfully wrought in the depths of the earth. God's eyes saw his unformed substance, and in Your book, O God, were written all his days when as yet there was not one of them.

This particular day happened to be the celebration that year of George Washington's birthday. So George went home after Eddie's birth and made a recording for his clients that day. "Yes, this is George's birthday," he said. "He weighed six pounds, four ounces and was nineteen inches long."

The recorder that day was maxed out with calls from all over the island. We found out later that people were calling their friends and telling them to call to find out the latest news. At that time, Hilton Head was a small community that knew all that was going on. We had message after message of well-wishers enthusiastic to hear the latest chatter. It was fun to listen to them.

Additionally, the other special thought of the day was the fact that George admitted to me that it was his mother's birthday. His mother had died when she was in her late forties, when he was in about the sixth grade. Since I had never known her, I was not familiar when her birthday was. When I heard that, I thanked God for her grandchild being born on his grandmother Lent's birthday. That was extra special! You not only give us the greatest gift that You could have in George Edward Lent, but You bestowed on us "abundantly more that we can ask or think" (Ephesians 3:20; John 10:10). Your grace and mercy abundantly flows to us!

11

Trouble Strikes

As soon as our son was born, I was wanting to hold him for the very first time. As I reached out to take him from the nurse, she retreated and ran out of the delivery room. I was shocked and dismayed that I was not the first person to cuddle him. I had had so much trouble finally receiving our first child who was alive and perfect.

The doctor immediately told me that she was superior in her nursing skills so that she may have seen something that caused her to rush him to the nursery. Well, that was not what I wanted to hear. I did not say anything to my doctor, but in my mind and spirit, I began to worry what was wrong with my newborn baby that would make her run to the nursery.

As the doctor prepared me to leave the delivery room and to be transferred to my room on the floor, he assured me that all seemed to be well for the most part.

When I saw my husband, I related to him what took place in delivery room. He said that they told him that he had some blueness around his mouth that had caused her to react in this way.

Since Eddie was born at six-thirty in the early morning, I had all day to contemplate his condition. I was not able to visit him in the nursery because I could not pick my head up off the pillow. The doctor had tried to give me spinal anesthesia, but the baby was too quick in coming for it to work. Then he called to me at the time of delivery to look at my baby, so I picked up my head. That was all it took for a severe headache to develop that day.

In the course of the later morning, the pediatrician came to see me about Eddie's condition. George was not there at that moment. The doctor began to give me statistics on why babies were born earlier than their due date. He indicated that possibly Eddie could have problems in his brain so that he came early. I was absolutely distraught! That was an understatement! I began to loudly cry.

As soon the pediatrician left my room, my obstetrician came to check on me. I explained what he had said. Without saying a word to me, he took off and did not return for at least fifteen minutes. When he returned, my doctor clarified the fact that Eddie was not showing any signs of brain deficiencies. He went on to elaborate that he had given the pediatrician a long speech about trying to frighten a new mother who had already delivered a dead child. He went to bat for me, and I greatly appreciated it.

George related to me that probably I did not need to view him at this point because he had tubes going in every hole available. The real problem turned out to be the fact that since he was premature, his lungs did not have a chance to develop completely before birth, and this caused difficulty after birth with breathing normally.

I prayed constantly in my spirit for our son that God would heal his breathing. Within three days, he snapped completely out of this problem. We were so very thankful.

At first, the pediatrician did not agree with my gynecologist about whether he was premature. Eddie's weight was six pounds, four ounces at birth. He looked huge against the very small babies in other incubators in the intensive care unit. After he saw the breathing problem in Eddie, the pediatrician agreed with my doctor.

The pediatrician ventured to say that Eddie would have weighed about ten pounds had he been born on time. He calculated his due date to be the first of April according to his breathing problems that he was having; yet he was born on February 15. He was about six weeks early.

After this time, they brought him to me, and I tried to nurse him. But, again, because he was premature, he would not suck very well. We both remained in the hospital for five days.

As soon as we left the hospital, I thought Eddie was eating well. Two days later, I wanted to be sure that all was thriving, so George weighed him on his baby scales in the veterinary clinic. I was horrified as his weight had dropped to five pounds, four ounces.

Immediately, we obtained a formula and began to feed him. His weight was regained in a two-week period.

One afternoon, I put Eddie in his bassinet for a nap. He slept longer than his feeding time. I went to wake him; he was lifeless, and around his mouth was blue. I screamed and jumped up and down on the floor so as to cause a disturbance downstairs in the veterinary clinic. George ran up immediately.

As he took him in his arms, he examined him, and the blueness had disappeared. He supposed he was in a deep sleep when I picked him up is why he seemed lifeless. Also, the afternoon shadows could have made him look blue, but was not. When he awoke completely, he seemed to be fine. However, this was very disturbing to a first-time mother!

After leaving the hospital, we decided that we did not want to keep Eddie's pediatrician from birth. I needed a doctor who was not an alarmist as the first one was. We then linked up with another pediatrician whom we kept through all our other children while at Hilton Head.

When Eddie was about a month old, George had asked me out on our first date since his birth. I was excited, but who would we trust with Eddie? My parents at this time were still living in Savannah, and both were working so they were not available to babysit. This would have been an hour's drive one way, and both had to be at work early the next morning.

We had established a relationship with one older lady in our church. When we asked her if she would commit to keeping him, she said that he was the ugliest baby that she had ever seen. I was horrified and shocked! That wasn't even what we were asking her.

Needless to say, she never, never ever babysat for us. That was the end of that relationship forever. To this day, I don't know why she thought she had to say that. As a brand-new mother, I thought my baby was the most beautiful baby I had ever seen.

One reason maybe that she was shocked to see him was most babies born at their due date had a larger frame than Eddie and especially had obtained more body fat than he. When he was born, he was nineteen inches long and over six pounds, but after losing a whole pound after coming home, he did not have much body fat on his bones. He did look very skinny for his length. Maybe I should explain that he looked emaciated. Still he was beautiful to his mom and dad!

As I went to my gynecologist for my six-week checkup after his birth, my doctor shared with me the probability of being able to conceive at a future time. Since this had been an issue for several years already, I was interested to hear what he had to say.

He started out saying that if we intended to have another child, we should not use birth control pills. He continued to say that my previous use of these pills had contributed to my not ovulating in my early twenties. At that time in history, these pills were very strong. In fact, they were much stronger than they needed to be.

He suggested that we not use any birth control to see if my body now would start functioning normally concerning ovulation. His further comments suggested that if we chose to use the pills again, and I proceeded in age before we tried to have another child, I, possibly, might not be able to conceive again at all. We definitely wanted other children, so we took his recommendations and did nothing to prevent another pregnancy.

Thank you, God, that You shower Your children with abundant blessings. Furthermore, in Deuteronomy 28:2, we find that God does not just merely give blessings, but that he wants to actually "mug us with blessings." He desires so aggressively to bless His obedient children that He runs us down, overtakes us in order to bless us.

Please imagine with me for a moment! God has all these presents in heaven, wrapped up beautifully, and waiting patiently for us to ask, seek, or knock for them. He is a good Father and desires to impart these blessings to His children (Matthew 7:7–11).

He not only blesses with children, but He blesses in many other ways—spiritually and temporally. God sees to it that His children "don't lack any good thing" (Psalm 34:10), and God also "gives us all things richly to enjoy" (1 Timothy 6:17). Praise His mighty name!

Remember, "the mercy of the Lord is from everlasting to everlasting on those who fear Him, and His righteousness to children's children, to such as keep His covenant, and to those who remember His commandments to do them." (Psalm 103:17–18) Praise Your name, Lord, for Your mercy and blessings to our children and our grandchildren when we obey Your Word!

12

Eddie's First Few Months

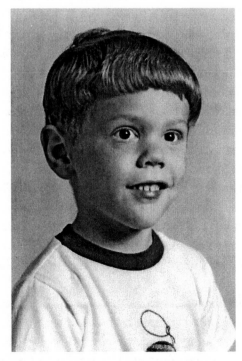

This is a picture of Eddie about 5 years old.

As the months progressed after Eddie's birth, his weight caught up with his growth. He was looking proportionately like a normal-sized baby for his age with his length and weight. They seemed to be balanced now.

He was an active young fellow always trying to scoot everywhere to explore new things. At that time, there was a very low-to-the-ground, almost flat scooter that had contours to fit a baby's small torso. This allowed a very young child to use feet and hands to push themselves along to go wherever they chose. Eddie loved this device. He spent many hours daily at different times during the day to explore his surroundings. As he reached the age to crawl, we put this device away until the next child.

Another neat creative toy that we bought for Eddie was a bag that zipped on the top to keep the water inside. It was a small fish tank that he could look into as he played in his playpen or bed. It could be easily moved from one place to another. He was intrigued by this fish, until one day when he could sit up and stand, he unzipped it, and I found him playing with the fish in his bed. Well, that was the end of that until the next child came along. We bought many Creative Playthings that kept him busy.

Just about a month before the summer was to commence, we had Eddie's first photo shoot at three months. I took him to Savannah to a photo studio to have lasting pictures of all different poses. As this was our first living child, we wanted to remember each growth spurt, so the pictures were numerous.

After taking these pictures, Eddie and I went to the Savannah airport to welcome my brother back from Vietnam who was a pilot in the Air Force. What a wonderful reunion that day. My sister-in-law and their young children had prepared a reception at their house. We all went there to eat lunch and visit and hear many stories. After lunch, we all left and allowed them to have fun as a family to truly reunite.

Our cousin had also been in Vietnam at the same time. He was a chaplain in the army. He came home a short time after my brother as he was trying to adopt a little girl from Vietnam. He had to wait on the paperwork to be completed before he and his new daughter could come home. Later that summer, we went to visit them after he also returned.

In the summer 1971, when Eddie was only four months old, we took him on his very first trip to the river to go crabbing. Marti and Ray, George's sister and brother-in-law, had come over to catch some seafood for dinner.

I had a large beach umbrella that unfurled above Eddie's playpen. We were able to easily stick it into some soft sand close to the river's edge. We brought his playpen that had a mattress-like pad on the bottom. Being out in the fresh air and the warmth of the sun's rays, he slept most of the time while we were catching crabs.

Now that we had the provisions to go down to the water with Eddie, we had many trips to the beach that summer. He seemed to enjoy the outside's warm air and the sound of the surf brushing the shore. As he was able to sit up this summer, he played at the water's edge in the sand and water.

As the months progressed into autumn, Eddie was growing and developing totally normally. We were very pleased with our new pediatrician. In the previous winter after Eddie's birth, He had a hard time when I had to stop trying to nurse him. The formula did not agree with him. We had used almost every kind of formula until we found this new pediatrician. He had told us to change the protocol of foods that we were feeding him. Many of those foods were causing allergies in him. When his body was used to this new regime, he began to thrive.

When Eddie was about seven months, we traveled to Disney World in Florida for a vacation. Our friends joined us for a fun-filled day. We had enjoyed many of the attractions all morning. As lunch time approached, we started searching for a suitable restaurant. Since we had walked all morning for many hours, we wanted to sit in a cool air-conditioned restaurant where we could relax and rest our legs.

When we approached the restaurant of choice, we saw a dwarf-sized man handing out rings advertising this restaurant. We requested that he not give Eddie a plastic ring so that he would not be able to put this in his mouth. He complied, we thought.

After waiting for about thirty minutes for a table, we sat to enjoy our friends and talk. I sat Eddie in a high chair next to me at the table. As our friends were talking, I glanced at Eddie. He seemed to be struggling as if he were gagging. Without saying anything, I jumped up to help him.

When I realized that I could not release him from the seat belt straps for the high chair quick enough, with one hand, I hurriedly turned the high chair upside down with Eddie still strapped inside. The other hand immediately went in his mouth. It was only an instant when I was able to pull that ring out of his throat. All that was accomplished in a matter of seconds, even before George or our friends had time to help. When I glaced at them, their mouths were hanging open speechless. The other people in the restaurant began to clap as I sat Eddie down once more. I held up that ring and they understood what it was about.

George and our friends were amazed that in a matter of seconds all was well again. They could not understand how I picked up that high chair with Eddie in one hand and retrieved the ring with the other. I explained when a mom sees her child in distress, adrenalin takes over and mighty feats are accomplished with the power from God.

Thank you, God, for your gift of children. I know that they are a special gift straight from heaven. You have so mightily blessed us with this child, Eddie. We are so very thankful that you have seen fit to bless us in this way.

There are blessings for all those who fear or have reverence for the Lord. In Psalm 128:1–4 God tells us "Blessed is everyone who fears the Lord who walks in His ways. When you eat the labor of your hands, you shall be happy, and it shall be well with you. Your wife shall be like a fruitful vine in the very heart of your house, your children like olive plants all around your table. Behold, thus shall the man be blessed who fears the Lord."

Also in Psalm 112:1–2 God proclaims to us "Blessed is the man who fears (or honors) the Lord, who delights greatly in His commandments. His descendants will be mighty on earth."

Thank you, Lord, for blessing your children, especially in this way.

13

A Second Blessing

After I had George Edward Lent, my doctor told me that if we wanted another child, we should not use any birth control. So we did not use any. We knew that we wanted to have at least one more child.

When Eddie was very young, we were particular about not trying to have another baby so that we could have some space between two children. As Eddie reached the age of nine months, we were getting tired of worrying about whether I was pregnant or not. We were not planning another child yet, but the Lord had other plans.

As Christmas reached us that December, I began to wake up every morning with nausea and a desire to stay in bed. I felt sick. After several days, I told George that I must have a stomach virus. He looked me in the eye and said, "I think you are pregnant!"

"What? Could I truly be pregnant! My heart considered that this was impossible," I thought.

I had such a difficult time getting pregnant in the first place, but then after having our first child, apparently, my body, through God's healing, rehabilitated itself with the proper hormones so that I could conceive naturally. I could not understand the idea that I had gotten pregnant without having to take the medicine from the doctor. I began to praise the Lord and give Him glory for making it so easy to conceive a child. Praise His name! What a Christmas present the Lord gave us that year!

My mind began to race and wonder if it was another boy, or is it a girl? Oh, for joy that I might be pregnant! My heart wanted a little girl, just in case I would not be able to conceive anymore, but it truly did not matter.

I made an appointment with my doctor who had walked through the difficult days of not being able to conceive and through the early disastrous first birth. I was so nervous because these two children would be about eighteen months apart if all went well. I would have two very young babies especially close in age. But, of course, that was better than not conceiving ever again.

After the test was done, and I knew that I was for sure pregnant, I prayed every day that I would not lose this child, as I did our first. Horror struck at four months when I started to spot and even bleed. My heart sank, and I screamed out to God, "God, don't take this child from me! Please give us a healthy little girl who will grow up to love you."

My doctor was contacted, and I was told to come immediately to be checked. Since we lived at Hilton Head Island, South Carolina, and the doctor was located in Savannah, Georgia, we had an hour's ride. When he examined me, he did not see any reason that this baby itself had problems. He surmised that it was because of the incompetent cervix that I suffered through the birth of the first child.

I was instructed to stay in bed for a few days, and he would evaluate me again the next week. During the week that followed, I spotted many times, but it was mild. It seemed as though it increased as I stood up and walked around that I would experience the bleeding.

The next week, he explained that he would have to "sew" this child into the womb for the rest of the gestation period. I was horrified! That meant that I would have to be given an anesthetic for the surgery. I had not even had any medication during the birth of George Edward because I thought that it could be harmful to the child. "What effect would this have on a developing child at sixteen weeks?" I questioned. Fear entered my heart! "Would this child survive this procedure or not?" I wondered.

The doctor explained that if we did not perform the surgery, this child would not be able to carry through the whole nine-months of gestation. It may not be able to even develop to the seven-month stage, much less the whole nine months. "Oh, what would happen if she was born even at five months?" I conjectured. Horror clouded my thinking!

All these thoughts were bringing terror, dread, anxiety, and panic to my heart. I could not fathom the thought of having a premature baby and all the ramifications of that. As we prayed together about what God would have us do, we had peace about proceeding with the surgery. We thought if it worked properly, we would not have to be concerned about whether she would live until a viable age.

If it did not work, we knew that "God orders the steps of man; how then can a man understand his own way" (Prov. 20:24). God is such a Good Shepherd. He foresees where our steps will lead, and He will either open or shut the door. God sees the whole picture and knows all the ramifications of all our decisions. I praise Him for directing and orchestrating where we need to be and how we need to walk! Thank you, Lord!

The surgery was performed within a short period of time. We actually went to the hospital the next day. After the procedure was complete, the doctor ordered that I should remain in bed as still I could be for the first several days. Then I could get up and walk around but have periods of rest.

In the time frame that this procedure was performed, it was in its infancy stage in the United Sates. These surgeries had been done by a doctor in a foreign country, but my doctor was the first to perform this procedure in Savannah, Georgia, and one of the first in the United States. In fact, there was a reasonable chance that my baby was his first child on whom he had performed this procedure through his practice. He could not give me another story about where or when he had done this in the past.

I was released to return home after two days but had to return to my doctor in two weeks. At this returning, he examined me and discovered that the baby had *not* grown at all in those two weeks. He was alarmed but just asked that I pray that the baby would start to grow in the next two weeks. Oh no! Here comes that fear again! "Will I lose this child?" my heart was sad with the thought. I was surprised that he asked me to pray since he was Jewish and I was a Christian, but we both agreed that God was needed to help.

My prayers by this time were desperate! I cried out to the Lord with my whole heart every day, many times daily. I fought in prayer for the life of my baby. Since the doctor had thoroughly explained that if the baby did not start to grow very soon, he or she would soon die.

Also, he expounded on the details of the surgery. He was confident that if he performed this surgery again, he would administer a lesser amount of anesthesia than he did the first time. That is another reason that we thought that this baby was his first experiment for this procedure.

Every day from the time I left his office until the time I returned in two more weeks, I was on pins and needles. George and I prayed together fervently for the life of this child. We felt as though Satan would love to have the victory in destroying our child, but if possible, we would do everything we could to prevent that. Warfare praying was in order!

We discovered what we could from the Bible on the best way to pray. We stood on every promise that we could find that applied to our situation.

Now the day arrived for us to revisit the doctor. My emotions were running extremely high that day. I grasped the fact that this could be the day when we find out whether our baby either was already dead, or if he/she would be growing. "Was I prepared for either of these possibilities?" I reviewed. "No! I could not fathom the possibility of no growth, which would lead to death!"

"Oh, God, be merciful to us and our baby!" my heart prayed silently. We both realized that if this baby did not grow, it would die. We would meet him or her in heaven when we die, but that was not what either of us wanted. Of course, we wanted life on this earth for our little child. To be able to hold and see him/her was so strong in us that we could not comprehend anything else.

We both held our breath as the doctor examined and tested my body. He yelled out, "The baby is growing!"

I screamed out loud, "Thank you, God. You are so very good!" At last, we could both rest in the fact that it was developing and would soon be viable to hold and cuddle. I went back every two weeks after that time until birth. It seemed to be a prolonged pregnancy because of having to have my visits two weeks apart for the next six months.

This baby was due about the middle of September. At the middle of August, I began to have days that were filled with episodes of cramping and labor pains. I called my doctor, but all he would say was "Lie down and relax!"

Since I wanted the baby to be as close to the due date as possible, I rested and prayed each day for the grace to endure. The week before he/she was born, I experienced labor very often every day and sometimes in the night. I was not able to sleep well, so I was getting very tired.

I had one appointment where I was begging the doctor to let me have this baby right then, but he said, "No, we must wait until next week."

I thought that week would never end. Every day was a drag. Eddie was only not quite eighteen months and was very active on his feet exploring. He was wanting to go places and do things, or maybe it was me who wanted to go places and do things. To tell you the truth, I was bored!

We had many friends who loved to go to the beach with us. That was easy to do since we only lived about one-half mile from the beach. Most of that summer, my friend and I had been on the beach watching our children play together while we visited with each other.

The day finally came for another revisit to the physician. By this time, he and I were becoming friends who enjoyed one another. My doctor was old enough to be my dad. He had a daughter who graduated from high school with me. She was in many of my classes. I knew her fairly well. He always loved to hear about what we were doing and where we may be going. It was always enjoyable to visit with a doctor who knows more about your life than to just be a patient he sees once monthly. Of course, by this time, we had been through many soul-disturbing adventures together.

"The next week was possibly my last appointment before the birth of our second child, or was it?" I contemplated. "Could this be the end, and I would be able to hold our baby?" I hoped.

That day, August 31, 1972, dawned with a beautiful sunrise, and the birds were singing vibrantly in the crisp summer air. They seemed to be chirping "Praise God, from whom all blessings flow!"

My best friend and I had already made plans to go to lunch at our favorite restaurant because we sensed that this may be the day that I will have the baby. Praise God!

Together we enjoyed our lunch and a time of visiting that we stayed so long I was very late for my appointment. George was eagerly waiting at his office for me when I arrived. He let me know that he was wondering why I was so late. Oh, well! In my mind, I knew what the rest of the day would bring, and in one way, I was dreading the process but longed to see and hold the baby.

After the doctor examined me, he cut the stitch in my cervix and told me to go straight to the hospital, and he would meet me there. Labor started while driving to the hospital, so I knew that "this was the day"!

I was admitted upon arrival, but the doctor did not appear for several hours. When he did, he told me that he would go to a party with his friends, but he would be in touch with the hospital.

"Oh, by the way," he said, "it looks like you will have a boy!"

I immediately came back with my response, "Oh no, I know that it is a girl!" He asked how I knew that. My reply was, "I felt like God had assured me when I was about five months pregnant that it was a girl!"

"Well, I hope that you will not be disappointed when a boy comes out!" he said. I assured him that I would not be disappointed.

Upon his arrival at about ten in the evening, he wanted to administer the anesthetic for the birth. I let him know that I was not going to have that in my system because George's cousin had a baby who died because of too much medication given to the mother. My baby was not going to be affected by that.

He instructed me that he would allow me not to have any medication for pain *if* I would be silent. I agreed. He told me, "You may not scream!"

"Oh, what a comforting comment!" I sighed.

As the night progressed, the nurse could tell when I would have a contraction because she heard a tapping noise when I grabbed the rail of the bed to keep from screaming. My wedding ring would make a dull sound on the rail. She came in to check on me and proceeded to move me to the delivery room. I asked, "How did you know that it was time?"

She remarked, "We taped your ring on your finger so that you could wear it during the birth, and every time you had a contraction, you would grab the side rails on the bed. When I heard one ring tap immediately after the other, I knew that it was time. I was timing your contractions by the ring taps."

Off to the delivery room we went! As my doctor was preparing me for delivery, a doctor friend of his was at the door of my delivery room. I craned my neck to see him. As they talked, I found out that his patient was in the hospital, and she was only six months pregnant. Her doctor was not expecting her baby to live beyond birth.

That jarred my memory back to the months when I was wondering whether to have the surgery to hold my baby or not. At this point, I was so extremely glad that those days were over, and it was time for our baby to be delivered.

As the delivery was in progress, at one point, I shouted a blood-curdling scream! My doctor yelled at me, "Shut up!" So I obeyed and did not scream anymore.

As soon as the baby crowned and was completely free, my doctor yelled at me, "It *is* a girl!"

I replied, "I told you so!"

When the baby was delivered, my doctor yelled to his doctor friend at the door of the delivery room, "This surgery is worth it!" as he held up my cute but very short, wonderful bundle of joy! My baby was the first of many babies my doctor saved with this new surgical procedure.

She was absolutely beautiful! We named our darling, Deena Maria. She was the epitome of a beautiful cherub as she had very fat cheeks. She was only eighteen inches long but extremely pudgy. She weighed eight pounds exactly. She was about two weeks early according to the due date. The doctor remarked that her shortness could have been due to those two weeks that she did not grow. I did not care at that point. All I wanted was a healthy baby girl during the whole labor. God was gracious and gave me just that! Praise His name.

My husband and I were ecstatic! Now we had not only a boy, but a little girl! We felt very complete at this point.

Our God heals and restores dead things. In the past, my body seemed to have been dead as far as my reproductive organs were concerned, for I was not able to ovulate at all. I am reminded of the story about Abraham and Sarah as, they were well advanced in years, and Sarah had never been able to conceive even when she was younger. So now that they were well past the childbearing age, why should she consider herself to be able to bear a healthy, perfect, alive child now? She even laughed inside herself at the time that the three men appeared to Abraham and asked, "Where is Sarah your wife?"

At the same time, the men explained that "I will certainly return to you according to the time of life, and behold, Sarah your wife shall have a son." Sarah laughed inside of herself. I can't blame her, as she was not just old, but very old, and never had a child before this time. But one of the men spoke and said, "Is anything too hard for the Lord?" (Genesis 18:1–15).

Our God is the God of the impossible! Jesus told the rich young ruler in Matthew 19:26, "With men this is impossible, but with God all things are possible". Also, when Mary, the mother of Jesus, was told that she would miraculously conceive a son, the angel at the same time spoke of Elizabeth, who was very old and barren, would have a son in her old age. In fact, it was Elizabeth's sixth month already when that angel said "for with God nothing will be impossible" (Luke 1:34–38). Not only is God the God who heals, but He also performs what is beyond impossible to men.

God is the giver of all life! As He breathed into Adam the breath of life (Genesis 2:7), so He also breathes into us our life-giving breath.

> How precious is Your loving kindness, O God! Therefore, the children of men put their trust under the shadow of Your wings. They are abundantly satisfied with the full-ness of Your house, and You give them drink from the river of Your pleasures. For with You is the fountain of life; in Your light, we see light. (Psalm 36:7–9)

In John 1:1–4, God makes it very clear that Jesus is the Word of God, the Creator of the world and the giver of life.

This picture is when Deena was about four years old.

14

From One Thing to Another

When we brought Deena home from the hospital, Eddie was only eighteen months old. He was running around everywhere as he was extremely active. He could talk very well for his age. He certainly was "Mommy's little helper."

He would dart from place to place, gathering what Mommy had just said. If I needed a diaper, he would be back in a moment with my request from the stack of diapers. He was compliant and helpful. He loved his little sister!

During that fall, I realized that Christmas was coming, and I wanted to make many of my Christmas presents. I loved to sew, and so I went to the fabric shop and purchased material. That year, I made aprons for the women in my family with their names embroidered on them with the help of my sewing machine. Yes, of course, I was very busy, but I would get bored if I only had to take care of children. While they were sleeping, I would get out my sewing, and that renewed my spirit and relaxed me. It was a refreshing diversion to being a busy mother.

When Deena was young, I thought that we would not have any more children. We had a boy and a girl, and that seemed like that would be sufficient. All of my friends were holding their children down at two. That seemed to be the popular concept among young couples. "Us four and no more" was the watchword for that time!

During the next few years, I started having major problems with my back. I went regularly every week to my chiropractor for relief from severe pain. That lasted several years and never seemed to be a solution as every week I had to go, because the pain would increase.

During those years, I did some fairly distinctive treatments to try to help this pain. We had heard of a new treatment to help the lumbar spine to move back into its correct position without going to a chiropractor to be manipulated. We bought some unique boots that would attach to monkey bars so that I could hang upside down in order to allow my back to fall back into place.

The first time I tried that, I was supposed to hang there for about twenty minutes. As my head dropped below my heart, I felt the pressure of my blood feeling as though it was pooling in my brain. Twenty minutes was far too long with that feeling. I was only upside down for a bare few minutes when I realized that I could not get down without help. I called loudly for George to come, but since I was in the far backyard and he was in his clinic in the front part of the lot, I had to wait beyond my capacity for patience for help to come and get me down. Now I knew for sure that this maneuver was impractical to do without a second person available at all times. What an awful stunt that was! Why did I even think that it would be practical and work! "Oh, well! Back to the drawing board!" I thought.

When I spoke to my chiropractor about how these boots were a waste of money, he suggested that I borrow his unit where you could hang upside down only enough to hopefully put your vertebrate back into position, but not enough to cause pain in your brain by hanging completely upside down for twenty minutes.

We moved this unit into our house and used it for several months. This did seem to relieve some pain for those many months. It did not cause me to have a headache from the blood pooling in my brain and not returning to the other parts of your body. With this stunt, I did not have to turn completely upside down. I was able to experience relief in my back from partially hanging not quite upside down. I was able to function better doing this procedure than anything else. Praise God!

My mother was a huge help during those many, many months the pain was increasing. She came over almost every day to help with the children and play with them so that I could rest in bed to also get relief. As my dad had already passed away, this also helped to fill a void in my mom's life also.

The problem that was the worst was the fact that nothing was completely alleviating this pain. The severity of the pain was increasing with each month. I soon was not able to vacuum the house at all without having to be in bed for several days after the fact. My mom, by this time, was doing not only the housework, but taking care of the children. I became unable to do much of anything.

I first went over to Savannah to seek an orthopedic doctor to do a myelogram to see if I had a ruptured disc. After having this test, the orthopedist reported that I did not have a ruptured disc. So this left me with no solution.

I knew that something had to happen to change my life. I, one day, decided to fast for God to answer my prayer about what I needed to do to solve this dilemma. I went over to the church next door when I was fasting so that I could concentrate on being able to listen and hear God. I read my Bible and prayed many times for different requests all having to do with this pain. I particularly asked God to help me find a doctor who would be able to know exactly what was wrong and what to do about it. I asked God, "Lord, if I find the right doctor, please, have him say that he knows exactly what my problem is and that he has a solution!" I knew if the doctor said what I said, this would definitely be the doctor whom God chose.

As I prayed longer, several things began to unfold. First, an orthopedic doctor came to the island to live. Secondly, the Hilton Head Hospital opened its doors for the first time ever. These two new occurrences took many months for them to come to fruition.

I became the first patient of this orthopedic doctor. He followed my situation for many, many months. He ordered several tests. After all these tests were complete, I had no recourse as yet because this doctor did not have a hospital in which to practice at this point. Nothing more could be done if I was going to continue with him.

15

Another Step Toward Progress

Because Hilton Head Island was growing by leaps and bounds, numerous kinds of doctors began to establish their practice of medicine on the island. It was a lucrative opportunity for many kinds of professions among younger couples.

Most of these doctors were retired from their lifelong practice of medicine in other places. Hence, doctors with much experience came to establish a hospital. Many other doctors came who were young and full of energy and were guided by these older professionals. Our medical community grew almost overnight to be a strong force to keep us all healthy, from the youngest to the oldest.

The hospital site was chosen by these professionals with the advice of real estate agents. It was set to be located on the north end of the island where we lived. At this time on the island, it was the day of the volunteer for whatever job needed to be done. Volunteers were summoned to clear this land so that progress could be made to start the building. Since we owned a tractor, George volunteered to begin to clear this land. He was one of many who came at different times to do a little here and a little there.

As the building began to come into being, many inspectors were on the job to guide its development for completion. George was the official and only fire inspector on this end of the island. He was summoned several times to keep tabs on the progress from a fire standpoint.

As the hospital was slated to open, he was summoned to inspect this facility. He went over each inch of this building, checking on how safe it was against fires, and to make sure there were open exits in case of fire. He found between twenty-five and thirty problems that did not give a good report.

As he made a report as to what to change, they seemed to laugh at his authority. Some of these complaints should have carried much weight, but no one was listening. He even asked several nurses at work there if they knew what to do in case of fire. They all acted as though they had more things to do than consider what to do in case of fire. They finally went to the governor of South Carolina who waived these problems as being of no consequence. They obtained their certificate of occupancy. We were glad that we did not have to use this facility until these problems were corrected.

When it first opened in 1975, they had a fire alarm that had a Morse code of beeps to figure out where the fire would be. These beeps were so confusing that the firemen and hospital authorities were unable to determine where the source of the fire lay.

They thought that it was the roof. After searching the roof for about twenty minutes, that was incorrect. Finally, someone came up with the idea that it was the incinerator out back of the hospital. From that, the hospital personnel realized that they needed to be more alert to fire problems than they realized. This was an embarrassment to the administration personnel who should have known more about that fire alarm.

After it opened, many doctor's offices opened around this complex. We had many kinds of doctors a person would need. In the orthopedic department, the doctor who helped establish this hospital made arrangements for the head of neurosurgery in New York City to come down for a week to do many surgeries that were needed.

I was called as a possible patient because of all my previous symptoms with my back. I again fasted and prayed that God would move in this regard. Again, my prayer was, "God, if You want me to do what this doctor is recommending, have him say 'I know exactly what is wrong with you, and I can help you'."

The next day, I went for my appointment. He reviewed all of my test results and said, "I know what is wrong with you, and I can help you!"

I was shocked at his response and surprised in my spirit! "But why was I so stunned when I had asked God to specifically answer my prayer? I asked, and He answered! Why should that be so astounding?" I told myself.

He went on to explain that he could tell I had ruptured a disc many years prior. It seemed as though this old rupture was causing severe symptoms.

I, then, remembered that I was diagnosed by a doctor in New York state that I ruptured a disc. I had forgotten about it until this was brought up. In the summer of 1964, I spent six weeks at Chautauqua, New York. During my first week there, I was washing my hair in the kitchen sink in order to hurry so that I could go off with my friend. Just as I had wet my hair, I had a horrible pain in my lumbar spine at my waist. My friends had to help me to the bed. The next day, my housemother obtained an appointment with a local orthopedic doctor to examine me. As he checked my muscle response at the knee, he reported that I had ruptured a disc. He explained that since I was young, this probably would heal itself in time. I continued to stay at Chautauqua but had to remain in bed a lot. I could do some things but had to rest in between. I still enjoyed my stay there and continued with my courses that I was taking.

That day, I had asked the neurosurgeon why the doctor in Savannah told me that I did not rupture a disc. After repeating the myelogram, this neurosurgeon explained that when he did another myelogram, my spinal canal was larger than the doctor would have expected it to be. Through his experience, he put more dye than usual in it. When he did this, the rupture showed up plainly.

The surgery was scheduled for that week. After this procedure was performed, the doctor reported to us that because of this old rupture, scar tissue had started to trail down the sciatic nerve that was allowing impulses to my lower leg and foot. Since so much time had elapsed since that original disc had ruptured, much scar tissue had formed. This was causing these increasingly severe symptoms.

At the time of surgery, this scar tissue was carefully scraped from my sciatic nerve. When I first stood on my feet after the surgery, my leg gave way because this nerve needed to heal. I walked with a walker for the first week in order not to fall. After that, I was good to go and not fall.

After this surgery, my body took about six months to a year to regain all my movements without pain. I was fully restored after a year.

Praise God that you are Jehovah-Rapha, the God who heals. Healing of any kind comes from you, and you alone. Even the wisdom that doctors have comes from God. God is the source of all wisdom and answers. Since he is all-knowing and has all the answers, He is the author of all the questions. So seek Him, and Him alone, for your medical needs. He may send you to the doctor for help, or He may heal you Himself. That is up to Him!

16

God Has Other Plans

As my back healed, and the severe pain finally subsided, we were anxious to have another child. After having received a clearance from my orthopedic doctor, I commenced to become pregnant again.

At this same time, our church had just lost its pastor. For a second time, we contacted the Evangelical Institute in Greenville, South Carolina, for a possible pastor possibility. At this same time, George had been praying about going to Bible school at this facility.

Mr. Carroll, the director and founder of this school, agreed to pray about the direction for our church. After a few weeks, he contacted us to inform that he had a possibility of a new pastor. We talked with him about us attending his school for two years. At this time, we were giving a fleece before the Lord to see what God had in mind.

When this young man from this Bible school agreed to be our next pastor, he was married a few weeks before this time. They both moved to Hilton Head as a young couple.

A few days after he moved with his wife to the island, my friend, who had not met him yet, invited all of us to eat supper with her family. Her family consisted of two sets of twin girls, a single boy, and her husband. The first set of twins was identical, and the second set was fraternal. They were thankful that the third pregnancy was not twins.

I arrived at her house slightly early, as the children wanted to play on the beach a little while before supper. I was standing at the edge of the surf, looking toward her house when I saw our new pastor coming. I told her not to turn too quickly as he would know that we were talking about him. I then told her that I would move where she was so that she could turn around and see him. She exclaimed, "He's just a boy!" I quickly retorted, "But that *boy* surely can preach!"

That night, we all got to know this new pastor better. We all became friends with them over the years. Her family had more opportunities to fellowship with them than our family did because God led us to Greenville, South Carolina, to the Evangelical Institute.

My friend and her family became very close to this pastor. If she thought that he was not preaching something correctly, they would discuss each issue. She had been a Bible scholar for a very long time. As they discussed each issue, they became closer and closer. It was a very healthy relationship in the Lord. They both grew in the Lord due to this "iron sharpening iron" (Proverbs 27:17).

This speaks of how when we both search the Word in order to discuss a truth from God's Word, both parties will benefit from this study and discussion in the area of character and knowledge of God's Word. Each will then realize why they believe or do not believe a certain truth. They will, again, in time be able to give this new knowledge to someone else in the future. It will cause both parties to search the Word and turn to God for answers. Not only do they grow together in fellowship, but they will grow together as friends in the Lord.

Since the church was thriving under this new pastor, God led our family away from Hilton Head to Bible school at the Evangelical Institute in Greenville, South Carolina.

CHAPTER 2

I Shall Not Want.
Psalm 23: 1b

There is no want to those who fear Him . . . But those who seek the Lord shall not lack any good thing. (Psalm 34:9b, 10b)

But let patience have its perfect work, that you may be perfect and complete, lacking nothing. (James 1:4)

Let our people also learn to maintain good works, to meet urgent needs, that they may not be unfruitful. (Titus 3:14)

17

A New Life in Greenville— Our Third Blessing

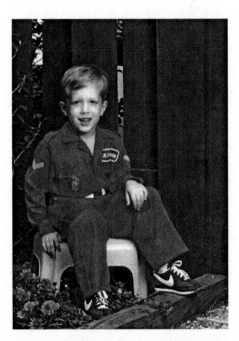

Here is David, age 5, in his fireman outfit.

In the summer of 1977, God firmed in our heart that His will was for George to be a student at the Evangelical Institute in Greenville, South Carolina. At this time, we had two children who were starting kindergarten and the first grade. What's more, I was early pregnant, so I would not be available to attend all the classes.

The verse that God had used to move us was Matthew 6:33: "Seek ye first the kingdom of God and His righteousness and all these things will be added to you." God promised here that if we would seek Him first in our lives, He would provide the everyday things of life.

Our first hurdle was to secure a veterinarian to manage our veterinary practice those two years that we would be gone from Hilton Head. George made one phone call to a former veterinary student whom we knew who had worked with him. This student had since graduated and moved to Savannah to work with another veterinarian there.

George explained to his friend the situation. His friend was eager to leave the veterinarian in Savannah and work by himself in a veterinary practice. This would be like working for himself without having the cost of buying a practice. This young man was very excited for the opportunity. Thank you, God, that we only had to make one phone call, and this position was filled!

Our next hurdle was to secure a decent place to call home in Greenville. George and I traveled there with the children to register him at school. While we were there, George and I had looked around that section of town for a house, to no avail.

When we met with Mr. Carroll, and he prayed about the house that the Lord would provide, he had a specific prayer straight to the point: "Lord, give this family the house of Your choosing that will meet their needs today!"

He prayed with us about this request and then proceeded to go to look at various houses with us. The first house we looked into had just what we ordered. It was even on a dead end street so that the traffic would not be a problem with the children playing outside. The house was high atop a medium sized hill so that the children were not in danger of going down to the main road at the bottom of it. It even had a room for George to use as his study. It was located within about two miles of the school, and it had three bedrooms, two baths, and a large great room that flowed from the kitchen, dining area, and into the living room. A sizable picture window adorned this living area, and another one was located in our bedroom. The living area overlooked a wooded area that led to the street, and our bedroom surveyed our grassy backyard. It was perfect! We secured it on the spot. We returned to Hilton Head to make the final arrangements before the move.

Our family began packing for our new life in Greenville. This feat was significantly larger than I had expected. It was almost as distressing as a complete move. Not only did we have to bring all our furniture, clothes, toys, etc., but we had to clean the house in depth that we were leaving in order for this veterinarian to relocate in our house.

As I have mentioned before, we were expecting our third child. I was between two and three months pregnant in August 1977. This was my fourth pregnancy, and since I had major trouble with the surgery that caused me to have a cervix that would not hold a child to term, I was instructed to lie down and rest during the course of a day. This move was taxing my body with the strenuous sorting, packing, cleaning, and moving. My doctor had warned me that this could cause a miscarriage. He had already given me the name of a doctor in Greenville who would be able to "sew my cervix" tight at about three months.

After all items were safely in our moving trailer and the children and us were in our car, we set out on our six-hour drive. We arrived later on the afternoon of that same day. I was exhausted, as well as the children.

We moved at least some of our major items into our house that night. It was a wonderful change from a small two-bedroom apartment with two children and two adults.

As I walked through the house the next morning, I realized how large it was with sparling rooms that floated one into the other, which gave you a very spacious feeling. The living area floated into the kitchen and the other end into the front hall. I love a house that is not chopped up into small rooms in which it would be hard to maneuver.

The big picture window looked out into the street and wooded front yard so that I could keep up with the children when they were playing outside. Our bedroom also had a picture window that overlooked the fenced-in backyard slowly climbing up the hill. It was easy keeping up with our dog in the backyard.

At the end of the cul-de-sac at the top of the hill, there was an empty house for rent. I began to pray that another young couple would move into it with children the ages of our children. Well, it was not long when we saw movement in and around that house. I kept my eyes peeled for the people who possibly would be moving into it.

Finally, I was able to make contact with them. The couple was the same age as ourselves, and their two children were also. One child was a boy who was the same age as Eddie, our son. The next child was a girl who was exactly the age of Deena, our daughter. They all became fast friends. They enjoyed these children for two years. God is so good to answer our prayers specifically!

When it came time for George to start classes in Bible school, he felt as though he needed to be able to exercise every day to balance the time of sitting in class and at home studying. His solution was to ride his bicycle to and from school every morning and every noontime. His classes were over by noon and in some afternoons; he had to work at school. It was about a two-mile ride from home to school. The only problem with the ride is that he had to cross four major lanes of traffic that was a main thoroughfare. I cannot believe that I encouraged him to do that. I am glad that he survived those rides for two years.

As we settled the family into our new home, I began having major bleeding on a Friday night. I immediately went to bed and rested. That night, the bleeding subsided some. The rest of the weekend, I remained in bed so as to keep this bleeding under control.

On Monday, I called this new doctor and reported that I was having trouble. They saw me immediately. This new doctor told me to continue to rest and see what would happen in the next few days.

As the week progressed, some days were free of bleeding and others were not. I had in total three times of major bleeding that should have, and could have, resulted in a miscarriage. But God was so very gracious. I was able to maintain this pregnancy. While the doctor examined me at the end of the week, he scheduled me for the surgery that would secure the baby.

I was almost, but not quite, three months pregnant. This doctor went on to explain that if we waited for three months, I may lose this baby. The only hope was to complete the surgery then and not wait. We complied. After the surgery was finished, I returned home to rest until all the spotting had subsided.

This procedure secured this child for the remainder of the pregnancy. Thank you, God, that our baby was still alive at the end of this ordeal. My due date was the second week in March. I was able to have a pregnancy that was normal from that time forward.

The pregnancy was uneventful until the birth. My stitch was taken out at the doctor's office about two weeks before my due date. We were expecting to proceed to the hospital as soon as it was removed because that was exactly what happened to Deena at her birth.

We had a friend to take care of our children that night while George and I had a candlelight dinner at home. That night was uneventful. Because I did not proceed into labor, we picked up our children the next day. My mother was scheduled to arrive that afternoon.

After mother arrived on a Wednesday evening, we visited with her for two days. Friday night, we had a Sunday school class party for young couples, so we left the children with her as we attended. During this fellowship time, I started having cramps. We went out to our car to start it, but it didn't work. We were able to ride home with another couple that evening.

I slept well that night with no activity. On Saturday morning, I went to help George try to fix our car. He had plans for me to steer our car as he pulled it off with another vehicle. He explained that he wanted me to steer the car, but I should not put on the brakes for any reason. He said that his vehicle would slow down our car if we came to a stop light, but "don't put on the brakes for any reason!" he reiterated.

I was not too sure of that comment, but I agreed. He slowly pulled me off and was soon sailing down the highway at a rapid rate. I could see that we would have to stop at the light that we were approaching. In my mind, I would crash into the back of him because of the high rate of speed that we were going and the fact that the light changed quickly just before we arrived there.

I was terrified! "No brakes. No stop!" I mused. I held my breath and wondered how long it would take for me to plow into the back of him as he stopped. Somehow, we stopped without an accident. I don't know how that happened.

Since there were no other cars around, I got out of my car and proceeded to jump up and down to let him know that I was mad and upset with the situation. I jumped up and down as I screamed, "You will not do that to me anymore!" I was crying and yelling at the top of my lungs.

He got out and told me that he was sorry and calmed me down. By then, I had already jumped up and down enough to make the baby come. I felt very uncomfortable the rest of the day.

That night, I slept good, but in the early morning, I was awakened by cramps in my lower abdomen again. Without having my stitch in place and the fact that it had been about five days since it was removed, we headed to the hospital to be checked. With an incompetent cervix, you can have the baby extremely quickly and without much warning. There was a high rate of car births with this condition. We even had in our car an emergency kit for a car birth.

As we arrived at the hospital, my usual doctor was not on-call. His associate was the doctor of the day. He examined me and told us that this baby would probably not come until the next morning. Since my mother was showing anger toward me when there was not any reason for it, I did not want to return home. She was not showing it to the children, but to me. I did not want to go back home and listen to her fuss the rest of the day. She had already said if I go to the hospital, she would not go to church with us if we returned. She did not want to be embarrassed if we have to leave in the middle of the service due to labor.

The doctor suggested that he would help by inducing full labor that day. This was about ten o'clock on Sunday morning when he gave me the option of inducing. We both wanted it to take place on Sunday, as George was expected for school on Monday.

The labor progressed after the I.V. was started. My nurse admitted to me that this was her first day on the job since she graduated from nursing school. She was very pleasant and excited about her first delivery, but I was not looking forward to being attended by a nurse who did not have any experience apart from her school training.

George and I had brought the book *Practicing the Presence of God* by Brother Lawrence with us to the hospital. So, as the hours progressed, we were reading and practicing what Brother Lawrence was suggesting. At least, it kept my mind off my troubles.

During this time, I complained that I thought the labor pains were becoming too hard too quickly. I asked this nurse to turn down the drip while inducing labor, but she reported that the doctor had a wedding to attend at two o'clock that day, and he needed for me to deliver quickly. Had I known that in the beginning, we would not have chosen to stay.

So the drip continued, and I could tell that something was not right. I was in extreme pain. We progressed in a short time to the delivery room. My thought in my mind was "as soon as he tells me to push, I will push hard in hopes to deliver this child quickly, as the pains were terrible." I was one who had all the babies so far, naturally, without any medication for pain. This one was the worst pain that I had ever experienced. As soon as he said for me to push, I did.

I pushed extremely hard and delivered the child within several pushes. The doctor and the nurses left the delivery room, and we were alone with our son, David Joshua Lent. George picked him up from his little bed and held him as well as myself. We spent quite a while with him before the nurses and doctor returned.

As the doctor was examining me, he started cussing. I thought, "Why is he doing that?" I was about to tell him to stop when he reported that during the birth, not only did I tear on the outside, but the inside as well. The reason he left us so long in the delivery room, he realized, was that he needed another doctor to help him reconstruct the damage that occurred during this birth. When he obtained a helper for this situation, he returned and reported that he would have to give me medication for this procedure. I told him I wanted my husband in the room. He said that I would have to allow them to sew this up without any medication. I agreed.

It took them an hour to totally reconstruct this mess. Because of this situation, he missed the wedding. After it was complete, the nurse packed the site with ice packs to reduce the swelling.

All I cared about was that our child was safe and in good condition. I praise God that our handsome, David Joshua, did not suffer any damage himself.

By the time I returned home on the next Tuesday, Mother was in a better mood until it was almost supper time. For no reason that I could understand, she walked into my bedroom and announced "I am not fixing supper tonight!" George heard her say this, so he volunteered to prepare that meal. Neither one of us could ever understand why she announced that when the day had gone well. The next night women from our church brought several meals.

It snowed that day right after I was released from the hospital. It was enough snow that the next day, the children were able to go sledding down our driveway with Daddy. I could hear them having a wonderful time.

Being from the southern coast of Georgia, I had not had many opportunities to enjoy snow myself. I craved to be where it snowed. So I got this brainy idea that I would join them in sledding. This was the next day after being released from the hospital. I slid several times down the hill and walked back up this hill into the house.

As soon as I went to the restroom, I realized that I was bleeding again. I straightway went to bed and asked my husband not to tell my mother that this was happening. We never told Mother about that. I prayed that God would stop this, and I would not have to go back to the hospital. By the next day, it had subsided. I never went sledding after a baby again. Even when we do something stupid, the Lord still meets us in our need.

We had a wonderfully healthy baby boy who weighed seven pounds, six ounces and was twenty inches long. Praise God that He protected this tiny child during his first three months of gestation. In spite of all the trouble when we first moved, he was still perfect in every way.

This was new life for this family in Greenville—a new life in understanding about Jesus, and a new life for our baby. Since there were so many human errors in this story, we are so very thankful for the Lord's mercy.

Psalm 116:5–7 sums up our thoughts. "Gracious is the Lord and righteous; Yes, our God is merciful. The Lord preserves the simple; I was brought low, and He saved me; Return to your rest, O my soul, for the Lord has dealt bountifully with you." Additionally, in Psalm 136:1, 4, "Oh, give thanks to the Lord, for He is good! For His mercy endures forever . . . To Him who alone does great wonders, for His mercy endures forever!"

Thank You, God!

18

Three Things We Learned in Greenville

God was doing a mighty work in causing us to grow in grace and in the knowledge of our Lord Jesus Christ (2 Peter 3:18). What did Greenville bring into our lives?

1. *I observed the power of God in a particularly mighty way.* One day, I was bringing the children home from school with their friend, and we were stuck in traffic that was dead still. I began to survey if I could change lanes. When I looked in my side mirror, all was clear at that second. When I proceeded to change lanes, a car hit us from behind. It was only a fender bender, but the police came to investigate. After the officer arrived, he instructed both of us to drive our cars into a nearby parking lot.

    Once we settled our vehicles off the road, I stepped outside of my car to speak with the police and the man who hit me. He accused me of pulling out right in front of him. The curious part about that was that I had looked in my side mirror, and no one was coming so then I changed lanes. He must have swerved out in anger in that split-second after I looked. Nevertheless, we had to speak with the policeman concerning what happened.

While the policeman was gathering his clip board to record the details of the accident, I started witnessing about Jesus to this man. As I found out he was a professor at a nearby university. It was not until I mentioned the name of the Lord Jesus Christ that this man literally jumped up into the air backwards in the parking lot. His body moved through the air many feet as I spoke the name of Jesus. This was astounding to me and the policeman! That day all of us saw the mighty power of God demonstrated! It was as if the mighty authority of Jesus' name picked him up and threw him backwards. Due to this incident, the policeman suggested that we all get into the officer's car to talk.

We both complied. While the man and I sat in the back seat and the officer in the front, the policeman started helping me witness to him. Between both of us sharing, we talked to this man about thirty minutes. I was very surprised!

After we spoke, he confessed that he was a Buddhist. I gave him a tract before he left. Praise God for the demonstration of the potent force of our God right before our eyes. After we both explained the gospel of Jesus, the officer started gathering the details of the accident.

I don't have any idea if that man ever became a Christian or not, but at least I communicated the gospel to him. Maybe I planted a seed or watered someone else's seed (1 Corinthians 3:8), but I do know that his blood will not be in my hands. (Ezekiel 33:1–9) I was obedient to present him with the gospel, and the policeman helped. It was only my responsibility to give him the gospel and God's responsibility to convict him so that he would come to Jesus.

> He humbled Himself and became obedient to the point of death, even the death of the cross. Therefore, God has highly exalted Him (Jesus) and given Him a name which is above every name, that at the name of Jesus every knee shall bow and every tongue will confess that Jesus is Lord to the glory of God the Father (Philippians 2:8–10; cf. Romans 14:10–12).

If he does not bow his knee in this life, it will be too late when the last time to bow comes. We must all pronounce that Jesus is Lord or Boss of our life, having a personal relationship with Him while still living here on the earth. *Lord* indicates that He is the sovereign ruler over all creation and things, such as people, animals, etc.

2)   *Eddie had opportunities in sports with other children.*

As I was taking Eddie to various places with his sports, we were filling up with gas more often than usual. One day I went by the gas station and realized that gas was fifty-four cents per gallon. I went home and said, "I will not pay that much for gas!"

Well, since there was nothing that I could do, I had to pay that, so I counted out our pennies and away I went to fill up. Our penny and small change collection helped us meet our needs more than a few times.

Eddie in his sports was learning how to be coordinated. He was on a T-ball team when he was in the first grade. He loved this activity at practice and was excited to participate. At his first game, however, he was the only child who "struck out" while trying to hit the ball, which was located on the top of a pole. He could not even hit the ball when it was sitting on a pole ready to be hit. Oh, well, I will have to admit that I was embarrassed that our son could not hit it when it could not have been in a better position. Mom had to learn that it was not important if he would win, but that it was important for him to have a good time while learning how to be coordinated enough to hit the ball. I will admit that I had to laugh when his bat, for the third time, missed the ball!

When he was in the second grade, he enjoyed playing football. Each of these little guys thought that they were so important as they ran around the field trying to figure out what to do. It soon was apparent that one boy on his team was fast approaching being their leader.

He seemed to understand quickly what to do to accomplish these things in a speedy way. He apparently had the gift of swift running. God seemed to have given this little fellow quite a natural ability to run speedily. His name was Beebo! Well, at least that is what he was called. He was the only black boy on the team, but all the children respected and loved him.

Beebo was often chosen to carry the ball down field. It was amazing to the parents how he could run that fast. We all looked at him in amazement. This team won every game that they ever played.

When it came time for the county championship game to be played, our team was the only team that had not been beaten. So that night came for this game to be played, and this is how it went.

All the children had to arrive early to be weighed in to make sure that each child was not overweight. As we gathered, the boys went one by one to his turn on the scales. When all of the boys on our team had been weighed, we thought, everyone realized that Beebo was not there. If he did not come, we knew what the outcome of the game would be. I began to pray that he would arrive shortly.

As I was praying, he appeared on the field just in the nick of time. As I observed, he did not have his cleated shoes on his feet! When he finished weighing, he related that he could not find his shoes, so his mother was still at home looking for them.

As the time was rapidly fleeting for him to be able to play that night, we were all waiting on pins and needles to see if his mother would find his shoes. Just one minute before the authorities were about to tell him he could not play without his shoes, his mother came running across the field waving his shoes in the air. "Oh, good, at least she got here before it was too late," I thought.

The outcome of that game was fabulous for our team because of Beebo. Since He was able to play, he could outrun any child his age and did so all throughout the game. He ran touchdown after touchdown. I will have to admit that it was fun for our team. They were awarded the county champions for the fall of 1978.

3) *The Lord put us through the fire to prove that he was sufficient to meet our needs.*

While living in Greenville, we had a major financial crunch. We went from having as much money as we needed to having barely enough to survive in Bible school. It was an odyssey that I would not have missed. If you ever want to prove the sufficiency of God, just commit your life completely to Him, and He will teach you (2 Corinthians 12:9). According to scriptures, it is *not* necessary for God's children to beg for bread (Psalm 37:25) because He will meet us in our need at that moment (Matthew 6:33).

A crisis that we were having at the same time is the fact that we only had twenty-five dollars per week for groceries for a family of four. Needless to say, I had to find a meat that was inexpensive. So I bought a lot of liver because it was only twenty-five cents a pound. This was the cheapest meat for us to purchase. Even to this day, our joke in our family is about joke in our family is about eating a lot of liver while we were in Bible school. The children used to sit for an elongated supper sometime before consuming their dinner. George and I happened to enjoy liver every now and again. But today if we are having liver, the children (who are now grown) will not come over that night.

We were fortunate that when we were having a crisis for food, a family in our church owned a refrigerated truck that carried frozen vegetables. Sometimes we would get a call. "Do you need any vegetables? Our truck's freezer has stopped working, so we need to get these vegetables to someone quickly," they reported. They would bring us many types of vegetables to eat that day. We lived for these times as they had a variety that we could not afford. We ate well countless times on their vegetables.

Another person in our church also drove a Pepperidge Farm truck. If he had bread that did not sell, he gave us the day-old bread at the end of his day. Often, he would have many loaves of party-rye bread that he would give us. People would not buy this size bread as much as the standard size. The children thought that these tiny sandwiches were so cute. They loved the taste of rye also. It made our mealtime more interesting and fun.

Additionally, the veterinarians that George worked for began to call him to work for them in their clinics on Saturdays because they wanted to go to football games of their favorite teams.

He worked for two in particular, which allowed him to work for them so that they could have time off many Saturdays. This came in handy for us since we had limited funds coming in from Hilton

Head. God met our financial needs many times from the income from the Saturday work. Thank you, God!

Remember the verse that God used to initiate our odyssey to Greenville was Matthew 6:33: "Seek ye first the kingdom of God and His righteousness and all these things will be added to you." We literally did not have enough money to make ends meet each month, but God provided in one way or another. George was truly seeking God first, every day and all day.

Furthermore, close to the end of George's first year at school, we were confronted with the fact that the veterinarian that was running our business wanted to return to Savannah soon. We were horrified as this meant that we might not be able to complete the Bible school, and the children would not be able to continue in a Christian school. We would have to return to Hilton Head.

As we prayed for God's guidance as to what to do, God impressed George with making another phone call to secure a veterinarian. This time it was to an acquaintance that George had met in veterinary school. When he called him, we found out that he no longer was in veterinary practice, but for the last year, he had gone to seminary to study God's Word. He related to George that his school had not done what he thought it would—it had not taught him the Bible.

George, then, presented him with the opportunity to return to veterinary practice by taking over our veterinary office. He told George that if he had called yesterday, he would have turned him down, but the night before, this man had decided to leave his school. He accepted on the spot. Thank you, Lord, that You allowed George to complete his Bible school! This second veterinarian accepted our offer without ever seeing the Hilton Head office. He was so desperate to leave his school and return to veterinary medicine that he accepted without understanding the details of our practice, but the Lord smoothed out the rough spots.

Since the first veterinarian wanted to leave as soon as our first year was completed, We went back to Hilton Head for one month in the summer until the second veterinarian could get there. Because we had to relieve the first veterinarian as soon as possible, we left all of our belongings in our house in Greenville, except for clothes, and we then enjoyed four weeks at the beach. The children and I were thrilled!

Since June was one of the best months in the veterinary practice, we made a significant amount of money to take back to help us through the second year at Bible school. This certainly was a sizeable gift from God that we did not expect. Thank you, God! Even the event that appeared to be terrible turned out to be a blessing in disguise. Remember, "all things work together for good for those who love the Lord, who are called according to His purpose" (Romans 8:28).

As we learned about the power of God and His sufficiency in every situation, God taught us that we should turn around and declare His power to others. In the story about God bringing the plagues in Egypt while Moses was asking the Pharaoh to let the children of Israel go, we see the magnificent power of our sovereign God. As God was about to bring the seventh plague on the Egyptians, He declared, "For this purpose I have raised you up, that I may show My power in you, and that My name may be declared in all the earth" (Exodus 9:16). Isn't this true for us today? God desires even today that in us, he will show His power through us that His name might be declared and glorified. Great is our Lord and mighty in power (Psalm 147:5) for God rules by His power (Psalm 66:7).

In our entire life, God means for us to live by God's sufficiency, not ours. Remember that everything we have comes from God alone: "Not that we are sufficient of ourselves to think of anything as being from ourselves, but our sufficiency is from God" (2 Corinthians 3:5).

This is a picture of Eddie when he was in the second grade while
we were in Greenville. Thanks to "Beebo", his team was the county
champions in the fall of 1978.

19

Three Additional Lessons from Greenville

1)   *Humiliation had its place in perfecting us in Jesus.*

Mr. Carroll would purposely humiliate his students in order to help them to properly react to various events that would be difficult. There were a handful of times when Mr. Carroll deliberately tested all his students with humiliating situations and expected them to respond in the correct way. For a while, we wondered why Mr. Carroll had been so hard on his students about giving them difficult situations in their work detail, but after a while, we figured it out.

He had been on the mission field for many decades before the Lord led him to found this Bible school. He knew all the pitfalls that missionaries face on the mission field. Because of this, he strived hard to prepare his students for whatever situation they would face. One way to help students to react properly when under an authority was to make them be under the authority of someone who did not know what they were doing or having an authority who was treating them harshly. During their work detail time, the students had no idea what kind of situation they would have each day.

George and a younger friend were told by the school to go to an older woman's house to cut her grass and do her yard work. They both complied with joy. While at her house, she treated them as though they were teenage kids out to do a good deed, as if they did not know how to do anything. George, at age thirty-five, as a veterinarian with ten years' experience at this time, and his friend, who was in his earlier thirties, was a medical doctor with almost as much experience. She called them "boys," and she acted as though they did not know how to do anything, so she supplied the directions in a very demanding way. If she had gone to her local emergency room that night, she would have found George's friend as her doctor. Or if she had taken her pet to the veterinarian on Saturday, she would have found George as her pet's doctor. But she made them feel they were incapable of this difficult job. They complied with every request with respect, even when they knew an easier way or a better way to accomplish these tasks. She was very a demanding and angry person.

Also, a more humiliating experience was when George and his friend had to be under the authority of a young man twenty years of age who knew nothing about putting up fences in the country. He was a city boy with no prior experience. This young person was ten to fifteen years younger than either of them. He began to explain how to construct a fence that George knew was not going to stand very long. But George and his friend listened to this younger person and followed his instructions only to have to go back the next day and reconstruct this very fence the way they knew best.

God is not looking for us to make a great fence the first time, but to have the right attitude with your authority and to try to make your authority successful if possible. Many times in life, we all have to comply with requests from authorities that are not always the best way, but God still has an authority structure that He expects us to respect.

Understanding the story about the Roman centurion who had a sick "servant that was lying paralyzed and fearfully tormented"

(Matthew 8:5) is of great importance. Jesus was willing to come to his house, but the centurion remarked that he "was not worthy for Jesus to come under his roof" (v. 8). The centurion went on to express how he understood authority because he had many soldiers under him. When his authority said go here or there, they go and do accordingly. "When Jesus heard this, He marveled! Jesus said 'Truly I say to you; I have not found such great faith with anyone in Israel'" (v. 10). Jesus instructed him to "go and it would be done *as he believed.* And the servant was healed that very moment" (v. 13, NASB). So it pays to stay under your proper authorities in any situation.

2) *We were confronted with compellingly powerful preaching.*

Moreover, because of Mr. Carroll's preaching being extremely strong, it gave us a chance to examine ourselves to see if we were truly in the faith that we thought we had. Since George heard his preaching every day, he soon became unsure of his salvation. George took himself through the process of salvation and committed his life to Jesus again. He even drove a pole in the ground in our back-yard at Greenville to commemorate that day. This would forever remind him that he was saved for sure on this day. Satan is always there to make us doubt salvation if we allow him since he is "the father of lies" (John 8:44). Satan also wants to steal, kill, and destroy anything in a Christian's life (John 10:10). So "stand against the wiles of the devil" (Ephesians 6:10–18) and "fight the good fight of faith, lay hold on eternal life, to which you were also called and have confessed the good confession in the presence of many witnesses" (1 Timothy 6:12).

I never doubted my salvation, but his preaching made me want to delve into the scriptures to make sure that I was not a pretender in the Lord (Matthew 7:21–23). In this passage, the people highlighted here were doing all kinds of wonderful activities for the Lord. They were passionate about what they were doing. But they lacked one thing—a personal relationship with Jesus.

After they gave all their credentials for knowing Him, He said to them, "*I never knew you!*" (v. 23). They failed to have a relation-ship with the One whom they were serving. We must all have a personal relationship with our Lord. Some people also want to do good works for Him, but they never have received the One who gave His life and died for them (John 1:12). It is not important that we "say" we know Jesus; it is important that Jesus says that He knows us! (2 Corinthians 10:17–18).

3) *God taught us His Word and who we are in Jesus Christ.*

George attended and graduated from this ungraded Bible School. He took advantage of all the classes possible there.

Also, we had a wonderful church. Our pastor had great messages all the time. We learned much from him. Also, we had many friends there as the people were very loving and kind. The first year, I had my time of worship and prayer to the Lord when the children were in school. During this year, I attended a Bible study of one of the ladies in our church. This is where I was taught to memorize the Word of God in large portions. I memorized the first chapter of Ephesians during that year. I still remember it today. This set me memorizing other large portions of scripture through the years such as Genesis 1:1-2:3; John 14 and 15.

Also, the second year in Bible school, I went to some classes. Mr. Carroll was teaching this particular class where we were studying A. W. Tozer's book *The Knowledge of the Holy*. He would call on me "every single day" to tell how God spoke to me about the lesson for that day. I had to make sure that I studied this book and had sought every truth that God wanted me to learn from His Word before I came to class.

At first, I thought that he was calling on me because he saw me sitting up front, so I decided to move behind someone the next day. Secondly, I realized that, that was not the reason because when he could not find me the next day, he called out my name to locate me. He always expected me to share my word from God with the younger students. This kept me on my toes!

In America, people seem to fight against the authority structure. Everyone lives as though they know better than anybody and will not listen to their authorities. God has an authority structure in the home, church, work, and in the world.

The dad is the head (Ephesians 5:23; Genesis 3:16, cf. 2:23–24) with the mom as the heart of the home. God expects the children to obey their parents (Ephesians 6:1, cf. Luke 2:49–51). Romans 13:1–7 is a passage about authorities. The church has the pastor as the head and the other church authorities under the pastor. They should all be respected, and we all should submit to their authority.

But at the same time, these authorities in the church should be in complete submission to God and also take to heart what the people of the church think about different situations. The authorities in the church should not come across as being a "god" for the people.

We should have the same idea at the workplace (Titus 2:9, 1Peter 2:18–25). In the world, city or county officials, policeman, firemen, ambulance attendants, etc., all need to be submitted to when they are doing their jobs. "Obey those who rule over you, and be submissive, for they watch out for your souls, as those who must give account. Let them do so with joy and not with grief, for that would be unprofitable for you" (Hebrews 13:17).

Additionally, another area where a person needs to submit is in sports for the good of the team. At this school, volleyball was a required sport for all the students. George was in his late thirties while most of the other students were ten to fifteen years younger. George also had never been on an athletic team while growing up. He had never played any sport as a child. So he had a hard time being coordinated enough and to react fast enough for this game.

Most of the time, Mr. Carroll would assign George to be under the authority of a young girl. Mr. Carroll would say to the young girl, "Cover for Lent because he is missing all of his shots." So the young girl would come into his space and steal whatever was coming to him. This was frustrating to him. In reality, George was in better shape than most of them. He could beat them in the number of push-ups he could do and would be able to ride a horse bareback better than any of them. But that is not the point.

The point is that God is not interested in whether we know how to do something better than someone else, or how much experience one has above the other. He is interested in our reaction to the injustices around us. Do we accept help cheerfully and responsibly, or do we pout and react negatively to adverse circumstances?

The main and only purpose in life is to glorify God and tell others about His good news. In Galatians 2:20, Paul tells us, "I have been crucified with Christ; it is no longer I who live, but Christ lives in me; and the life which I now live in the flesh, I live by faith in the Son of God." Notice in this verse where it states, "I have been crucified with Christ." Of course, we are not literally killed with Him at the time of our salvation, but we figuratively died with Christ at the cross when we accept all that Jesus is and what He did. He nailed our sins to His cross and died in our place. In other words, He took my place and your place on the cross and bore the anger and vengeance of the Father just for us so that we will never have to bear it.

If we are truly dead with Christ and my selfish personal life has been given over to Jesus to be substituted by His life and His purpose, then what we do and how people treat us will not be the important matter. We will allow others to say or do whatever they like, and we will not react negatively, for we know who we are in Jesus Christ.

Remember, this life is to glorify God and not ourselves. "He who glories, let him glory in the Lord. For not he who commends himself is approved, but whom the Lord commends" (2 Corinthians 10:17, 1 Corinthians 1:31, cf. Proverbs 27:2). Also, "you were bought at a price; therefore, glorify God is your body and in your spirit, which are God's" (1 Corinthians 6:20). God will defend you when you need to be defended. You do not need to defend yourself! "May the Lord answer you in the day of trouble. May the name of the God of Jacob defend you" (Psalm 20:1).

Another verse that speaks to me in a major way is 1 Corinthians 10:31: "Therefore, whether you eat or drink or whatever you do, do all to the glory of God." This verse goes on to say "not seeking my own profit, but the profit of many, that they may be saved." Our life should be lived for the glory of the Lord and the profit of others (cf. 1 Corinthians 10:24). We are in the Lord's will, whether we are doing the duties of a pastor or a janitor cleaning bathrooms. We should do each of these jobs to the glory of God.

We all have to submit to one another (Ephesians 5:21). Women are noted for having to submit (v. 22; Colossians 3:18; 1 Peter 3:1), but in fact, we all have to submit to God and to one another in God's economy. In James 4:7–10, James underscores, "Therefore, submit to God."

Resist the devil and he will flee from you. Draw near to God and He will draw near to you. Cleanse your hands, you sinners, and purify your hearts, you double-minded . . . Humble yourselves in the sight of the Lord, and He will lift you up.

20

Fire and Ice

As I look back on our life, I have noticed that God has had "fire" throughout our lives. As a young married couple, George was the volunteer fire chief of the north end of Hilton Head Island in its infancy. At that time, Sea Pines and Port Royal plantations were just beginning to blossom. Palmetto Dunes was in predevelopment prices, and all the other plantations that now exist were not there as yet.

George was elected volunteer fire chief at the first meeting because he was the only young man who was present at that meeting. There were several older men, but they were looking for a young man who could go out and recruit the younger men and also have the energy to be a leader at all the fires.

So within the first year and a half of marriage, "fire" was a large part of our life. George was always the first one to be called. At that time, we had a phone system to alert the fireman. The department hired an answering service that called us, and likewise, we called another, and they called another. All the fancy calling systems that we have today were not in existence in 1968, at least out on the island.

Later, the fire department purchased a siren that was strategically placed atop the building so that the entire community would hear its sound and respond. Since we lived so close to the fire station, it would blast us out of bed in the middle of the night. Since George was the closest fireman to the house, he always was the first to arrive and take a truck. Usually, he arrived at all fires first.

In August of 1977, we moved from Hilton Head to Greenville, South Carolina, to attend Bible school. As we were inspecting the house, one aspect that we failed to notice when we first rented it was the fact that the walls by the heater vents in the living area were black with soot. I questioned the landlord as to what happened. She said that, in the winter, the house had an oil-burning furnace, and one day, that unit caught on fire, and the flames leaked out the vent into the living area and blackened the walls before it was extinguished. This caused me to be afraid of that system. The landlord assured me that it had been fixed since that time. We repainted the inside of the house while we were moving in so that we did not have to see this blackness anymore.

As we moved into our second winter, this heating system was giving us trouble. It certainly was not working properly. These memories of the previous fire that was described to us became very vivid in my mind.

One day, it would not turn on at all. We called the landlord, and she sent a friend of her family by to fix it. I was home with the children in the later afternoon when the man arrived. He was drunk out of his mind. When I realized that, I was afraid that he was going to set the house on fire as he tried to light it. He had not just been drinking a little; he could not walk straight at all or talk where you could understand him. I knew that his mind must not be working properly either.

My mind went immediately to the blackened walls. I gathered the children, and we all went outside the house while he tried to light it. Thank the Lord that he finally came to talk with me about the system because it would not light. He tried to explain to me what he planned to do in order to fix it. He was so far out in left field that I did not understand, and I told him to come back when he felt better. As a result, he then left.

Fear entered my heart at this time. Consequently, we contacted a friend. He came over to check out the system. He advised us that the system was too old to work properly, and it needed to be replaced. He remarked, "If it was not replaced, the house would burn down." Now fear was beginning to rage within me.

George called the landlord again and told her what we found out. She called another company, who came out that afternoon. They were not drunk! They seemed to be knowledgeable about these systems. They cleaned it, fixed a part, and lit it with success. All was well after that.

We went to Greenville in 2016, and our house was still standing, but hopefully, not with the same heating system.

After we moved to Clayton, Georgia, one of our chicken houses caught on fire and burned to the ground. Later we also had another time filled with fire that I have not as yet talked about. So I will save those stories for later.

When it comes to *fire*, I fear! And maybe rightly so. Nevertheless, *if* I am trusting God as I ought, I should not fear, "for He will be with me wherever I go", and no matter what happens (Psalm 118:6, Deuteronomy 31:6, Joshua 1:5).

If I were loving God the way that I should, there would be no fear in love. "Perfect love cast out fear, because fear involves punishment, and the one who fears is not perfected in love" (1 John 4:18, (NASB).

One definition of fear is *the absence of faith*. Faith in Hebrews 13:5-6 is an answer to this problem. "I will never leave you nor forsake you. So we may boldly say: The Lord is my helper; I will not fear. What can man do to me?" As this verse states, we need to *boldly say*! I will have to admit that fear is one of my strongholds that I have problems.

We all need to make up our mind ahead of time that we will not be shaken in the midst of life. When a storm of life is raging about us and we are caught in its frenzy, we need to resolutely stand and proclaim with boldness "I will trust in the Lord!"

Shadrach, Meshach, and Abed-Nego purposefully stood in the face of sure death (Daniel 3:8-30). They were going to be taken to the fiery furnace because they refused to worship Nebuchadnezzar as God. They had already, ahead of time, decided that they would only bow allegiance to the King of Kings and the Lord of Lords (Revelation 19:16). As the story is told, they walked around in this furnace with fire raging with a fourth man (Jesus Christ). The king called to them and they were delivered unhurt. They stood firm with an unshakable foothold in the Almighty, powerful God of all creation (Psalm 16:8).

Faith is believing God for who He is and what He has done for us. "Without faith, it is impossible to please God, for he who comes to God must believe that He is and that He is a rewarder of those who diligently seek Him." (Hebrews 11:6) Even in the face of death, we need to have our minds made up that we will not deny Him and we will stand for Him.

Praise needs to be the first words out of our mouth when we are confronted with any storm. Praising, especially in a crisis, has four benefits:

1. Praising brings spiritual health. In Psalm 103, *bless* means to praise and remember what God has done for us. When we remember who God is and what He has done for us, this builds our faith. When faith is increased, our feet will be set on a *solid rock* (Jesus Christ—1 Corinthians 10:1-4).

2. Praising brings deliverance. Praise helps us to soar like an eagle above the storms of our life and brings spiritual health and strength to our mind, heart, and soul (Isaiah 40:28-31; cf. Psalm 40:1-3).

3. Praising under affliction brings inward freedom. In Acts 16: 25-26, "Paul and Silas were praying and singing hymns". After a great earthquake, their chains fell off and the doors were opened.

4. Praising helps us not to forget all His benefits. Some of His benefits are forgiveness of sin, and recovery from sickness

(Psalm 103:3); deliverance from death; abundant loving kindness and mercy (v. 4); food to sustain life (v. 5).

Praising is one of the Christian's offensive weapons for spiritual warfare. A combination of praise and the Word of God coupled together and woven in each fiber of our life will be an invincible combination that Satan with his angelic demons will not be able to pierce.

21

One April Dawn

This is Rachel at age 3.

At the same time that we were praying in Greenville about what God wanted us to do after Bible school and we were preparing to visit Colorado for a month, God was also preparing us to receive our fourth child into this world, but we did not realize all of this at that time. On this tender, loving April dawn morning in 1979, God's will was made known to us.

As George and I were busy early that morning having fun, I screamed, "You are supposed to be at school in ten minutes!" He replied, "If you ride me in the car, I might be able to make it." So away we went in the car. I went as fast as I could and zoomed up the hill as students were running to class on the sidewalks. George usually rode his bike to school for the exercise, but because he was so late, I took him. Sometimes I don't know why I thought that riding his bike was a good idea because he had to cross four lanes of traffic to get to where the school was located. But nonetheless, he did that for two years and was still alive! Praise God! That day, it would have taken him too long to get there, and he would have been disciplined for it.

As I pulled up next to the school building, Dan Rulison (the brother of Jon Rulison) was always there, timing the students and reporting to the faculty who was late. If anyone were late, they got a consequence for being even a second late. That day, as George ran by Dan and he yelled, "You are thirty seconds late!" George tried to reason with him, but he would not listen, so George had to complete an extra work detail that afternoon. At least class had not already started.

The reason that the school was so tight on being late or arguing at volleyball time was because they said that in "real life," employers or others would be mean in some way, and we need to be prepared not to get mad and argue about situations but take criticism patiently. The volleyball court was their real-life situations, and you were expected to apply your spiritual warfare tactics to that period.

Six weeks later, I realized that I was pregnant. We were in Colorado when I was sure that I had conceived a child. When we returned to Hilton Head after graduation and the month-long visit to Colorado, I made an appointment with my gynecologist in

Savannah. He assured me that I was truly pregnant at the stage of three months. I began to spot shortly after that and had to be careful what I was doing. At this same time, the Lord was speaking and moving in relation to the beginning of the Christian school. I was involved with preparations for the opening of school.

Since school was to open the day after Labor Day 1979, we all were very busy making all the last-minute preparations for the first day of school.

When Saturday of that weekend came, the children wanted to go to the beach. Since we always tried to do fun things with them on Saturday afternoon, we made preparations to head to a wonderful afternoon on the beach.

When we arrived, George and I noticed that no one was at the beach. That was highly unusual since the sun was shining. Surely, there was not something that we did not know? As the children began to go into the water, the undertow was terrific. We both held on tightly to each of their hands. Finally, after about fifteen minutes, we decided to return home. One of our friends from Bible school, Bill Brown, was walking through our yard and asked us, "Where are you going due to the hurricane that is headed our way?" We both shouted, "What hurricane?" He said that the news was saying that Hurricane David was scheduled to hit the island about five o'clock in the "wee" hours of Sunday morning. We began making other phone calls and realized that this information was correct. He said that he and others from Bible school were headed to Elizabeth Gee's parents' farm outside of Aiken, South Carolina. When I talked with Elizabeth, she confirmed the information and invited us to go there also. We accepted the invitation.

Jon Rulison and George had to create pens made of plywood on the back of the truck in order for us to carry all the boarding animals with us.

After the hurricane hit Savannah directly instead of Hilton Head, we returned a couple of days later to find that electric and phone lines were down all over the area of Savannah and Hilton Head. I was scheduled to have had surgery to keep me from losing our baby the day after Labor Day. I was several days over that date by now. I tried to call and let them know that we had to evacuate the island on short notice. I found out that Savannah had worse damage than Hilton Head.

I received a call on the phone, but the connection was horrible. I could hardly understand anything they were saying. Finally, the person screamed into the phone, "Come to the hospital!" I knew then that it was the gynecologist's office trying to tell me that if I did not come, our baby would be in jeopardy because I was not able to carry a baby very long. I told George, and we had a friend babysit the children until my mother could arrive, and away we went in the middle of the mess to have the surgery to save the baby.

When we arrived at the hospital, we found that there was not any power. The generators were working to allow some lights, but not near enough to see clearly. It was hot inside as the air-conditioning would not work with the generators. I met with my doctor, and he explained that this surgery was an emergency because when a hurricane passes through the area, the barometric pressure would drop, and that could cause a woman to go into labor prematurely. As I was already experiencing bleeding, he scheduled that procedure immediately. As soon as the surgery room was ready, he proceeded.

As they rolled me into the surgery area, I was afraid for the life of our child. I was only four and half months pregnant, and the anesthesia could affect the baby's growth, as it did with our second child. I started to share with the anesthesiologist my concern, and she said that she would pray for me and my baby and would continue to pray during the surgery. She prayed and promptly put me to sleep.

The surgery went well, and I remained two nights to monitor the child's recovery. Everything was well, and we returned home.

The pregnancy went extremely well from September through January as I was busy with helping in the new Christian school. In the middle of January, I began experiencing labor contractions and pain. This continued until it was time for my next regularly scheduled appointment. I related to my doctor what was happening, and he said that it was time for the baby. He had me admitted to the hospital that day. But when I arrived there, the hospital was completely filled, and they did not have room for me. We waited in the waiting room for hours until my doctor came that evening. He made it clear that they would have to admit me so that he could induce full labor as he explained that if I went home and started experiencing the mild cramps that I had already experienced, this baby might be born at home or at least on the way to the hospital.

They admitted me immediately then and put me in a labor room. My doctor came in to talk with us as the drip to commence labor began. We enjoyed talking with him, but he also related the fact that he estimated that the baby would not be born until the next morning. He left my room and went home. He only lived about six blocks from the hospital, and he headed straight home that evening. As he was pulling into the driveway at his house, his phone in the car rang, and it was the hospital relating to him that I was ready to deliver! He spun around and headed back.

Meanwhile at the hospital, I called for the nurse as the doctor had just left. When she came, I told her that I wanted to push. Her response was, "Honey, I just checked you! You could not be ready to push. Remember the doctor predicted that your baby will not come until tomorrow morning." I looked her in the eye and screamed, "Push!" She immediately checked me and ran out of the room, saying, "Call Dr. Schneider back to the hospital."

As soon as she came back to me, they rolled my bed into the delivery room and settled me in that position. Also, they had called for an intern to stand at the door of that delivery room, waiting to see if he might have to deliver our baby. When I realized that he was there to deliver our baby, I started blowing and blowing as the Lamaze course taught me to do so that the baby would slow down and wait for my doctor. I thought, *No intern is going to deliver my baby!*

I kept blowing and praying that Dr. Schneider would hurry. I felt like I blew for an eternity. About that time, I heard his voice say, "What are you waiting for?" I yelled, "I was waiting for you." So I started pushing and boom! The baby came. The entire time from when I was admitted until when she was born was only two hours. That was the fastest birth that I ever had. After giving birth, I was told that there were no rooms available, and I would have to be put in a makeshift room with another girl for the night.

When the morning came, I could hear the voice of my doctor down the hall. He came in shortly after that and told me that I was going to be transferred to a private room in a few minutes. When I arrived at my destination, I was amazed at what I was given.

It was the father's waiting room that had been cleared, and a hospital bed was placed there with the proper equipment to have a patient. It still had all the couches and chairs, so when I had a visitor, there were plenty of chairs. This room was extraordinarily large for one room. It was also at the end of a hallway so that it was much quieter than any of the other rooms. I felt like a queen! The nurses related to me how my doctor pulled many strings to be able to arrange that for me.

I was extremely sad when I realized that evening that my baby was showing a high bilirubin. This meant that she was showing yellow pigment in her eyes and skin. She had to be placed under a special light that would help bring down this count. It stayed extremely elevated for four days. The doctors who were working with her said that if the bilirubin did not drop at all by the next day, they would have to do a transfusion. Dr. Schneider kept me informed as to what was happening. Maybe that first day, the doctors saw that coming and gave me a really nice room. We all prayed constantly and persistently that God would make it drop.

When the next morning came, I was waiting in fear and trepidation. When the doctor made his rounds, he shared that the bilirubin had dropped a very small percentage. I thought that they would still have to do the transfusion, but he explained that if there was any kind of drop in the numbers, that meant the baby would be fine and no transfusion. Oh, I started praising God! I also called my family and friends to thank them for their prayers and concern. We were able to go home that morning. By now, we were in the hospital for five days.

When I saw the baby that morning, she still looked very yellow. The doctors explained that I would need to put her in a window where the sun could shine on her often. When I did, the yellow color finally disappeared. Thank you, God!

We named her Rachel Anna, and she weighed eight pounds, four ounces and was twenty-one inches long. She was the largest baby that I was able to carry. Coming home from the hospital five days later, I made up a song just for her, "Little Rachel Anna, born in big Savannah," and this was sung in a singsong way. I was extremely excited that all went well after the first four days.

As David said in Psalm 34:8–10, 15, 17–19, 22

O taste and see that the Lord is good; How blessed is the man who takes refuge in Him! O fear the Lord, you His saints; For to those who fear Him, there is no want . . . They that seek the Lord shall not be in want of any good thing . . . The eyes of the Lord are toward the righteous and His ears are open to their cry. The righteous cry, and the Lord hears and delivers them out of all their troubles. The Lord is near to the brokenhearted and saves those who are crushed in spirit. Many are the afflictions of the righteous, but the Lord delvers him out of them all. The Lord redeems the soul of His servants, and none of those who take refuge in Him will be condemned. (NASB)

22

Many Opportunities to Do God's Will

As the time marched on in Greenville, George and I were praying about what God wanted us to do next. Since the Bible school had an emphasis on missions, our thoughts were that God wanted us to go on the mission field.

As George would go to the veterinary conferences every year, he would attend the veterinary missions program. We thought that God may send us out with them so that we could use veterinary medicine and a launching pad for our ministry. We prayed about this matter for many months.

At the same time, Mr. Carroll was meeting with his students that were about to graduate and was encouraging them to seek the Lord about placing them on the mission field in whatever capacity that He chooses.

With Mr. Carroll's prayers, along with ours, the Lord began to allow us to have many options. Mr. Carroll was considering us possibly to fill a request for a young couple to join an older missionary couple on the field in Japan. This missionary rejected us because we already had three children. He was looking for a young couple without children at this time. So this began to narrow down our prospects. Correspondingly, the veterinary mission began to fade into the background also.

We had three other possibilities that were in limelight of our minds; either go to Colorado where our friends were encouraging us to help them on his uncle's ranch with the cows, or to find a veterinary practice close to them so we could help them and work as a veterinarian. Similarly, the third option was to move back to Hilton Head and take our practice over again.

Since I have an adventuresome spirit, I thought Colorado might be the answer. The thought of going back to Hilton Head where there was not a Christian school for the children was a negative thought to me. As we talked with our friends, they were so encouraging that we thought we needed to at least go to Colorado to investigate.

George called the veterinarian who was at Hilton Head to discuss this matter. He wanted to hold onto our clinic at Hilton Head for the month of June 1979. George offered our clinic at Hilton Head as a possibility that he would want to continue there and buy this from us so that we could be free to go on the mission field.

As the dialogue continued over several weeks, it became clear that he had another possibility for a veterinary practice for him. His only request to us was that we would allow him to stay the month of June because his practice was not available until July of that year. We complied with his request because George wanted to research the Colorado possibility first.

The day after George graduated from Evangelical Institute of Greenville, we headed to Colorado to live on the ranch with our friends. We packed up our three children and ourselves and headed west. We were both very excited to be on a new adventure. We left our home in Greenville for the month of June but knew that we would return the first of July.

During this June, George worked faithfully on this ranch with cattle drives. I stayed with the children at the home site and helped prepare the meals for the crew of cowboys that worked with our friend.

We arose every morning at five o'clock on the dot. The men had to leave at this time to check fences and animals before they could start their day with duties near the house. I took the children from the house where we stayed to the main house, and they played with their children as his wife and I started to prepare a very large breakfast for the men to be served at seven o'clock.

We served an elaborate breakfast as the men were fasting until they returned home two hours later. It took my friend and me the entire time to cut, slice, prepare, and cook this feast for many hungry men, our children, and ourselves.

After the men ate breakfast, they began to work with branding new calves, giving vaccinations to other animals, or repairing fences in the back pastures. His wife and I had our later morning cut out for us with washing all the dishes by hand as they did not have a dishwasher and preparing to cook lunch for everyone again. Our lunches consisted of a large meal not just sandwiches. So, again, we had to wash a massive volume of dishes before the substantial supper meal was prepared. After the evening meal, another significant quantity of dishes had to be cleaned before bed.

One problem we were having was that when you live on the prairie of Colorado at five thousand feet, the altitude has an effect on your body. It makes you be extremely tired until your blood has time to adjust to this sudden change in altitude. One morning, we did not arise at five as usual. The men left George when he did not come for the cattle check that day.

I will have to describe our house to help you understand our situation. This house did not have any electricity in it. It was very dark as the windows were few and far between. At night, after supper, we went home to go to bed so that we would be ready for a full day starting very early the next morning and continuing until the evening.

One night, as we were starting to get ready for bed, I was standing in the doorway of our bedroom. I caught a glimpse of George coming toward me. I remained in the doorway waiting for my beloved to come to my arms. As I learned later, he could not see me in the dark. As a result, he plowed into me with bare feet and hit my shoes with his big toe. This resulted in the nail of his big toe tearing back to the quick of the nail. He was in pain in this dark house. I fumbled for the flashlight to investigate the damage. It was awful. Blood was everywhere. So much for my lover coming to me to hold me in this romantic moment, which, of course, ended with everything except romance.

The next morning, we slept in as our alarm clock did not work. The men did not wait on George, and they traveled out into the prairie without him. I did not show up to help with breakfast at all that morning.

As lunch started to approach, our friend decided to come to investigate what happened to us. As they were remembering that the house was heated at night with an unvented gas heater, they feared that something had happened to all of us. So he came over yelling for us to wake up. We arose with a start! We could not believe that it was as late as it was in the day. But from that day on, we felt as though we had more energy as we slept enough so as to allow our blood to adjust. For some strange reason, our alarm clock did not sound its alarm, or maybe we turned it off and went back to sleep.

Moreover, while we were there during the days, we investigated what our options were as working in veterinary medicine. We visited a veterinary clinic that was for sale. As we talked with the present veterinarian, we found out that he was tired of the late nights and early mornings in the bleakness of winter. He related that life on the prairie was hard in the blizzard-type snowstorms that they were used to. This did not make George want to consider this as a possibility.

Later in the trip, we visited the veterinary school to investigate the possibility of returning to school to learn more about cows and herds. But this seemed not to offer any good things for our family of five.

Besides investigating these possibilities, George and the whole family also went to Laramie, Wyoming, to attend a veterinary conference. The children and I became bored one day, so we decided to go to a museum. This museum had dinosaurs that entertained the children all morning. But I was getting tired of reading the information that they provided because it was all based-on evolution. Everything was millions of years old according to the writing. I was thoroughly disgusted by lunchtime. Since George was finished with his meetings for that day, I begged him to do something exciting.

We started investigating the possibilities of riding up into the mountains. On the map, we found "the snowy range" outside of Laramie. We traveled up and up the mountain until we reached this range. It was breathtakingly beautiful. We viewed the deep valleys and the snowcapped peaks that towered to about twenty-one thousand feet in the Rocky Mountains. Also, the rugged terrain of these mountains had a beauty of its own. We drank in the beauty of God and His creation. The snow was higher than the car on the sides of the road. Since this was the middle of June, we were shocked to find snow as we were not used to being that high up in altitude. The temperature up there was still very low.

The children were excited as they were able to play in the snow. We took pictures, as well as movies, of us playing in the snow the middle of June. It was a refreshing sight since we had spent that morning in a boring museum that did not consider God and all of His beautiful creation. But God showed us the real beauty in the afternoon.

The picturesque sights of God's creation were so breathtaking that it reminded me of when He first created the earth. "In the beginning, God created the heavens and the earth. The earth was without form and void and darkness was upon the face of the deep. And the Spirit of God moved over the face of the waters." As Genesis continues and the creation unfolds within the six days of creation, it shows the mighty acts of God and His ability to produce the most wonderful and ingenious world that we could ever imagine (Genesis 1–2:3).

How could anyone believe that all of this loveliness could have come out of the "big bang?" An explosion to my knowledge has *never* produced any order or beauty, only devastation and disaster.

Also, in the book of John, we learn that Jesus is the Word of God that created this universe as it was before the fall.

> In the beginning was the Word, and the Word was with God, and the Word was God. All things were created by Him, and without Him nothing was made that was made. In Him was life and life was the light of men . . .

and the Word became flesh and dwelt among us, and we beheld His glory, the glory of the only begotten of the Father, full of grace and truth. (John 1:1–4, 12-14)

Jesus, I do worship You and praise Your Name for creating all things by the breath of Your mouth. You truly are the fullness of the God-head bodily (Colossians 1:19; 2:9).

In this last few months of events, we went from fire to ice—Fire in the winter and ice in the summer. Lord, You have a very creative way to show your children lessons from Your Hand! Thank You, God!

The Medicine Bow National Park was part of the "Snowy Range" in Wyoming. This was June 15, 1979. You can see the snow on the mountain behind.

23

Moving Back to Hilton Head

After returning to Greenville the end of June 1979 from Colorado, we began to pack for moving back to Hilton Head permanently. The Lord had not shown us what to do in any other place than Hilton Head. I have to admit that I was less than elated about the move back. But back we went as the Lord had not given us any other options.

During the spring of that year in Greenville, George and I both were praying that God would move in order to secure a Christian school for our children. As the months progressed, it became the only possibility that was viable for us.

When we made this move back to Hilton Head, many of the young students from our Bible school moved back with us. About twenty young people infused the island with energy and enthusiasm, especially in the church. Some came to work for George in the veterinary clinic, and others were secretaries, teachers, mechanics, builders, etc.

Also, Mr. Carroll had been praying that God would supply someone to run the Christian school that God would raise up. After we returned to Hilton Head about two weeks into our move, my friend that had a child Eddie's age asked where I would be sending our children to school in the fall. Eddie and Deena were going to enter the third and second grades respectively.

Before I could even think of what to say, my mouth opened, and out of it flew these words; "We are going to send them to the Christian school that God will raise up." She remarked that it was now the middle of July, and there was not a Christian school on the island, so how was that going to be possible? I assured her that God would raise it for our children, as well as for other children. She could not see how that would happen in only a six-week period. To tell you the truth, I wasn't sure how that would happen either, but I did not say anything.

I went home and told George what she had asked and what my response to her had been. Neither one of us could really see how that would be possible, but we realized that we knew the "God of the impossible" (Matthew 19:26, Mark 10:27, Luke 18:27). In Matthew 17:20, in the second half of that verse, God reveals to us, "If you have faith as a mustard seed, you will say to this mountain, 'Move from here to there', and it will move; and nothing will be impossible for you." So *our faith* makes a difference in what happens in our life.

When our faith grows and we are learning to speak life-giving words, our life will be filled with twinkles from God. You probably are thinking right now, "What are twinkles from God?" I'm glad you asked!

Twinkles from God are moments in our life where we speak out of our mouth good, life-giving words that did not come from our own thinking but from the Holy Spirit of God moving in our life. Another way to express it could be that these "twinkles" can be times when we see the Hand of God moving on our behalf. Sometimes it is ever so slight, but it is there. We must be spiritually alert to catch these moments.

That day when I spoke with my friend, those were not my words but the words of God giving me a life-giving message that He was planning to bring forth. I was even shocked myself on what I was saying. All we have to have is a "mustard-seed-sized-faith" (Matthew 17:20) in order for God to move in our midst, and that "mountain" in our life would be moved.

God also gives us the "shield of faith" as a spiritual weapon to come against the evil one in our life (Ephesians 6:16). The evil one tries to come against every Christian to dilute our effectiveness in this fallen world. Satan is a liar and the father of lies (John 8:44). He wants us to believe his lies and allow him to build a "stronghold" in our life so he can have control of us. In 2 Corinthians 10:4, God exposes the truth in His Word:

> For the weapons of our warfare are not carnal, but mighty through God to the pulling down of strongholds, casting down arguments and every high thing that exalts itself against the knowledge of God, bringing every thought into the obedience of Christ.

Our faith is strengthened when we are in the Word of God, memorizing, meditating, and applying His Word to our life. Only God's Word can destroy "falsehoods or strongholds" that are built up in our life by giving into the works and innuendoes of Satan. Replace a lie of the evil one with the truth of God's Word, and you will live in victory to conquer these "strongholds" that Satan has built up in our life because of those lies.

About one week later, we received a call from Mr. Carroll reporting that he had found a headmaster for the school. He was a student who had become a teacher at the Evangelical Institute while we were there. In fact, he taught us the book of Joshua while George was in school. This man had recently been married and was willing to become the head teacher, as well as the administrator, of this new Christian school. He was friends with our pastor.

When Mr. Carroll had called about having a headmaster for the school, we had not even brought the subject up to our pastor yet. Nevertheless, our pastor never turned it down because it had come from Mr. Carroll instead of from us. He knew that Mr. Carroll was a man who walked with God and would not have sent him unless it was God's will. So because of the source of the solution, our pastor was willing to comply.

By the middle of August, our pastor Michael Baer and the new headmaster were on their way to Texas to be trained on how to manage this school. In the middle of August, they were on their way to get the training to use the Accelerated Christian Education program that September. They stayed in Texas for one week and returned fired up about making the physical preparations to our church. A special desk called a learning station had to be made for each child to do their work so that they could not see what the next child was doing.

One of the young people who came with us to the island that summer was Jon Rulison, grandson of Isabelle and Jon Kuhn (famous missionaries to China). He volunteered to make the desks in August so that the school would be able to commence in September. He had to make twelve cubicles since the Lord had moved in several family's hearts for them to send their children to our school that year. Wow! Twelve students were a lot for a brand-new school that only started within the last six weeks.

As the weeks progressed, the starting date for school was set for the day after Labor Day, 1979. When Labor Day weekend arrived that year, we took our children to the beach on Saturday afternoon and found that the waves and the undertow were horrible. We looked around and noticed that not even one person was there. As the children waded in the water, we soon saw that we would have to hold onto their hands to keep them from being washed away by the waves. We both decided that we should return home because of the danger to the children.

As we were walking through our backyard when we arrived home, one of the young men who had come back with us from school, Bill Brown, saw us and said, "Where are you going to escape the hurricane!" "What? What hurricane?" He related to us that Hurricane David was slated to hit Hilton Head directly before the next morning. Everyone has been told to evacuate as soon as possible.

"What! Evacuate?" we shouted. "But we have an entire kennel full of animals! How could we possibly take all the animals and leave? That would be an impossibility!" we pronounced in a chorus. But at the same time, we cannot leave them there with no one to feed them or allow them to go outside. All the owners of the animals began to call and say, "Don't leave my animal on the island when you leave." *What are we going to do?* we thought.

George and Jon began to brainstorm as to what could be done. George remembered some plywood that was in the garage that someone had donated to us when they were leaving the island many weeks before this time. God had supplied this wood ahead of time to be used now. Jon and George began building pens to fit on the back of the truck that would hold all the animals. That truck had belonged to my dad before he died in 1975. We had inherited it from him. "Thank you, Lord, for supplying the plywood and the truck for such a time as this (Esther 4:14)." I muttered.

They worked from that afternoon until about two o'clock the next morning when we pulled out of the driveway headed to a farm close to Aiken, South Carolina, that belonged to the parents of one of our friends who had come back after Bible school to live on Hilton Head. They graciously allowed all the young people from Bible school to stay at their place during the storm.

We were all glad that they were able to complete all the pens before five o'clock the next morning because that was the time that high tide was to occur, and also that was the given time that the hurricane was projected to hit Hilton Head.

As we started on the road, George, the children, and I were in our green station wagon while Jon Rulison was driving my dad's green truck with all the animals on the back. We were able to understand how Noah and his family may have felt with animals stuffed in the Ark. Our truck carried more than five animals in each pen. George had to think of what dogs would not fight with the other dogs and what cats would be best together. Everyone's animals were all mixed up together on that truck that night. I felt like we were the "ark" taking off just before the storm was to begin its major fury. Of course, it had been pouring for several hours already with a torrential rain.

As I watched Jon in the truck in front of us, he was weaving from one side of the road to another. We kept blowing our horn to wake him up because of his drowsiness. After about two and a half hours, we arrived at this destination. By this time, it was between five and six o'clock early that morning, and our hosts were in the yard, ready to help us get the children in and out of the rain and wind.

They were kind and thoughtful to us early that morning, when they were willing to have all the twenty young people, plus our whole family, for the next several days. They promptly put the children and myself in our room, and we all fell asleep.

George and Jon, however, were not so fortunate. They had to go to the nearby town of Aiken and meet our veterinary friend who had so graciously allowed us to use his kennel for the next several days (in fact, it was the same veterinarian who had managed our clinic the last year George was in Bible school). It was several more hours before they returned.

By this time, the hurricane was hitting Savannah at full steam ahead. I got up when they returned to try to call my gynecologist because I was scheduled to have surgery that next morning to secure our baby in my womb. I was able to call the answering service, which at that time was a live person who could tell you what you needed to do. As I was screaming into the phone because she could not hear me, she immediately hollered a terrifying scream, and the connection was promptly broken. Later I found out that the storm was hitting Savannah at that moment.

We stayed several days until the rain had stopped and the trees in the roads were cleared. Before we left there, we found out that the storm not only hit Savannah directly, but it circled around inland and hit the town where we were also. At least it slowed down somewhat by the time it hit us. This was still terrifying for the children even when it hit the farm.

On the way home, we all went to pick up the animals and head back to Hilton Head, not knowing if we had a house left. The damage was extensive to phone and electric lines, trees in roads and yards, but the house was still standing. George got the children and me settled in the house, and he promptly began cleaning up various disasters outside the house.

Due to the damage on the island, school did not start that year for another week. When the day came that next Monday, the students were excited along with the teachers. Wow! What an undertaking in such a short time! It was amazing to all of us that the Lord had done a mighty work to cause this school to arise from nothing to having twelve students and two teachers in place in a seven-week period. Praise His name!

The year progressed well for teachers and students. What a miracle the Lord did in our midst! Thank you, Lord!

God has the power to do what He knows is best by Himself if He chooses, but God does not desire to do that. He elects to use people to accomplish His tasks that He does on this earth. If someone is not willing to be used by God, He will move onto the next person to accomplish His will. Always be willing to be used by God when He moves in your life. Be sensitive to the promptings of the Holy Spirit (Luke 12:12, John 14:26, cf. Romans 15:13).

Just as it was in the days of Moses, God opened the Red Sea, and they all walked across. So it was in our day. God did our "impossible" task, and we walked through it in a seven-week period.

God is still also doing miracles today.

> I shall remember the deeds of the Lord; Surely I will remember Your wonders of old. I will meditate on all Your work and muse on Your deeds. Your way, O God, is holy; What god is great like our God? You are the God who works wonders; You have made known Your strength among the peoples. You have by Your power redeemed Your people. (Psalm 77:11–14, NASB)

You are still a miracle-working God! Thank You!

Also, just as God did "signs and wonders to be done by their hands" through Paul and Barnabas at Iconium, so God did "signs and wonders by the hands of all the people" He called at Hilton Head to set up this school in a seven-week period (Acts 14:3, NASB).

Hilton Head Christian Academy is still in operation thirty-eight years later. For a few years, we lost contact with anybody at the school. Two years ago, we received a call from the school. They were very interested in us giving them the details of its founding.

This year in March, we had the first Founders' Day. The families that were involved in its founding and the building of their present building were invited to attend to meet the board and encourage them to keep moving forward. We related that we only started with a handful of students, twelve to be exact. Now they have almost four hundred students from kindergarten through twelfth grade. The students put out a magazine every quarter and mail it to us. It is so very good to keep abreast of the activities and goals of the school. Lord, it was and is truly Your hand that has upheld this school all these years. Praise Your name!

CHAPTER 3

He makes me lie down in green pastures; He leads me beside quiet waters. (Psalm 23:2)

Oh, love the Lord, all you His saints! For the Lord preserves the faithful. (Psalm 31:23a)

Who then is that faithful and wise steward, whom his master will make ruler over his household to give them their portion of food in due season? Blessed is that servant whom his master will find so doing when he comes. (Luke 12:42-43)

Well done, good servant; because you were faithful in a very little have authority over ten cities. (Luke 19:17)

Now may the God of peace Himself sanctify you completely; and may your whole spirit, soul and body be preserved blameless at the coming of our Lord Jesus Christ. He who calls you is faithful, who also will do it. (1 Thessalonians 5:23–24)

Come unto Me, all you who labor and are heavy laden, and I will give you rest. Take My yoke upon you and learn of Me, for I am gentle and lowly in heart, and you will find rest for your souls. For My yoke is easy and My burden is light. (Matthew 11:28–30)

24

Be Still and Know That I Am God

Here is our family with "country in our heart" and
with our animals living on the resort island of Hilton Head.

God's hand again rises to show us the way He has chosen for us. We lived above the clinic on Hilton Head for more than eighteen years. As the older two children were getting to the preteen and teenage years, the island was growing rapidly. To give you a picture of life at Hilton Head, our oldest son used to ride our horse down a backwoods dirt road to the Pizza Hut, get our pizza, and ride home. He would tie Red our horse, to a tree outback of Pizza Hut by the dumpster, get the pizza, and return home.

While living on the island, many people were consumed with social climbing. Their perspective was on wealth, what plantation you live on, or who had the nicest car and house, etc. I was getting very tired of that.

As I have pointed out before, while on Hilton Head, we had many friends whom we brought back from Bible school with us. They spread out through the community to work. Some were secretaries for businesses, others were construction workers or a mechanic, more were teachers in the Christian school, but several worked with George in his veterinary practice.

My friend Judy was one of those who worked with George in the veterinary clinic. Judy was a very faithful worker. She always arrived to work on time and stayed late should the need arise. She was unmarried at that moment.

Judy and I prayed together every day during the week for one hour. Since George and I only lived upstairs above the veterinary clinic, it was easy for her to meet with me each day during her lunchtime. Judy always ate her lunch during surgery time so that she was free to pray at her lunch hour with me.

Judy and I prayed for more than five years because there is one prayer that I prayed for five years. I can't remember exactly how many years we prayed together in all, but it was many.

My prayer was that God would give us a farm in the mountains. I do not know why I was praying that. Here we were at Hilton Head with a very lucrative business, the beach within less than a mile from our house, and George was involved in many organizations that were ministry related. Therefore, our life was complete and fulfilling.

Every day Judy and I prayed five days weekly. I would put the children down for a nap or allow them to read a book in order for us to have a quiet time while we prayed. This prayer was in my heart in a powerful way. I could not get this thought out of my mind.

I did not even know where this farm was to be. As I began sharing this prayer with George, he was *not* impressed. He related that he was very satisfied right where we were and had no intention of moving.

Nevertheless, I was not daunted in my efforts. God had apparently placed that thought in my heart, and it was not easily taken away.

Despite George's efforts to tell me that I was being used by the devil to dissuade him from doing God's will, I relentlessly kept praying. Year after year, month after month, day in and day out, I was faithful to this prayer.

After a while, George began to ask various people in the veterinary clinic where the best and quickest place in the mountains would be. Nine times out of ten, people would invariably say this one town—Clayton, Georgia.

I had a friend from high school who would come down from this town to Bluffton, South Carolina, to see her aunt. We would get together every time she would come. One day, I asked her where in the mountains would a nice place be for us to live? Her response was also always the same! It was where she was living in the mountains—Clayton.

All of a sudden, this place was in our constant thoughts. We had never been there but began to desire to go to see what it was like.

As each year passed, the veterinary business was affected by other veterinarians coming into the area. The business was up and down depending on the latest veterinarian who came on the scene. One of the later veterinarians who came opened his clinic not far from where we were located. That one affected us more than the others.

George was also tired of hearing about this farm. So when the older children were fourteen and twelve and a half, they went on a retreat to Greenville, South Carolina, with the Christian school for a long weekend. The next week, they were out of school for the spring holidays.

George grew so tired of hearing about this farm that he decided to go look for it. He knew that would be the only way to silence me. He thought, "We will go look for the farm so that when we don't find it, she will be silenced forever."

I was excited that he was willing to spend one week looking for it. On that Sunday, the children were going to be taken back to Hilton Head, so we picked our older two children up before they left. We spent that night with our friends and had plans to leave that Monday morning.

So away we went on Monday morning to set out in search of the farm in the mountains. We had told our friends that we would be back on Wednesday evening to their house because we had to return to Hilton Head by the end of the week.

We looked around Greenville during the weekend with our friends, but nothing seemed right. Away we went out into the countryside with no specific direction, except for the fact that most people said that they would go to Clayton for a nice mountain experience.

We were driving on all the back roads from Greenville toward the mountains. All of a sudden, we were at a crossroads. We could either go to the right or to the left, but a choice had to be made. The sign said Cashiers, North Carolina, to the right, and Clayton, Georgia, to the left.

George remarked that he did not have a veterinary license in North Carolina, but he had one in Georgia. So off to the left we went toward Clayton.

On our trip, we were camping along the way to save money on motels. Of course, the children loved to camp and were excited. As we woke up and made breakfast, we always would have our family devotion. Each morning, I would constantly pray that God would show us the farm in the mountains. My prayer that last morning was "God, if you don't show us the farm today, I will never mention farm again!"

Our aim when we arrived at our destination was to find a real estate person and look around. While driving, we would pull in by a sign and casually look at the property but would ride on without talking with anyone. *But God* had other plans!

As we drove into the one community, called War Woman to the east of Clayton, at every "for sale" sign we saw, we would drive in the road and glance at the house but would always move on. Until we saw one sign that intrigued us so much that we had to stop and back up.

I had spotted a cute little house with a sprawling pasture as its front yard. I made George back up and pull into this road. As we drove down the bumpy dirt road, there was an old rickety bridge that we were going to have to cross. George remarked, "There is no way I will cross that broken-down bridge with a fifteen-passenger van with four children and two adults!"

At that moment, I realized that there were two mothers watching their several children playing down below around the creek. I got out and talked with them. I told them our objective of the week, what we were looking for, and then I asked if there was a Christian school in the area.

As soon as I mentioned *Christian school,* that struck a chord with the lady who owned the house. She invited us up to their house and said that her husband was at home that day, and he might be able to help us.

When I told George what she said, he remarked, "I am not driving this van over that bridge."

I said to him, "The lady said that she would drive it over for you if you wanted her to do that."

He said, "No, I will drive it over myself!"

We drove up to their house and met her husband. He was plowing the field to plant a spring garden. It was April 3 to be exact. He stopped, and we all went to their house for homemade cinnamon rolls and ice tea on their front porch.

The friend of the owner of the house was not friendly. She sat in a rocking chair with her arms crossed and did not say a word. Later, when we became friends, I asked her what she was thinking. She said, "I was afraid that you would hurt us or steal from us! In fact, I thought you might be the ax murderer!" Of course, we had no intention of either of those activities. Later, the unfriendly one became my best friend, and we are still friends.

As George shared with the husband and his wife, the husband said that he knew someone who had two places for sale. One was a large house that would be great for our sizeable family, and he had a chicken farm where we could make a living.

The one thing that George knew we needed for our family was a way to make a living from the place that we would buy. The large house that could hold our family was beautiful and perfect in every way except that we would not be able to make a living from the land as it was only six acres.

George mentioned to the owner that we were told that he also had a chicken farm for sale. That man lit up and said, "Yes, I do have a chicken farm for sale, but I will have to go back to town and get my truck before I will take you out there."

So we all went back to town. He picked up his truck and began driving us out to the farm. The scenery was beautiful, with rolling hills and beautiful pastures that soon turned into mountains. We drove for about twenty minutes when he stopped, and he shared with us that this was the starting of the farm. As we drove down that small-country bumpy road in the middle of nowhere, we stopped and gazed with wondering eyes at the beautiful sight of rolling green pastures with eight chicken houses that were working and a small house.

This was the last day that we had to look for the farm, and by eleven o'clock in the morning, God showed us His farm that He had picked out just for us! I was very moved in my spirit by the awesome sight, but at the same time, I was nervous that I had conjured this up, and it was what I wanted and not what God wanted.

George was very excited when he saw it because he knew that he could make a living by raising chickens while trying to start a veterinary clinic. He was convinced that God had chosen this for us, and he was interested in finding out more detail about the business end of this farm.

Our family walked the property lines of the farm as the owner worked with his chickens. The farm was about 125 acres, including mountains, rolling hills with an ample supply of pasture land, eight working chicken houses, and one house that had only two very small bedrooms.

I made a statement that I regretted later! I said, "Don't worry. I don't care what the house is like because we will build another one soon. That was a mistake!" Another house was not built for many years later due to a financial crunch.

Wow! Thank you, God, for placing Your desire in my heart and then fulfilling it in Your time! It is so exciting when God takes you on a journey and makes His will so plain to you. In Psalm 27:7, 14 (NASB) David shared, "Hear, O Lord, when I cry with my voice, and be gracious to me and answer me." But the hard part was when we had to wait so long for Your answer. Then God told us to "wait for the Lord; Be strong and let your heart take courage; Yes, wait for the Lord."

One of the hardest things to do is to wait for the Lord to supply, no matter how long we have to wait. God reminds us in Isaiah 40:31 "Those that wait for the Lord will gain new strength; they will mount up with wings like eagles, they will run and not get tired, they will walk and not become weary."

Always be sensitive to the leading of the Holy Spirit. Listen for His still small voice that speaks to His children. (1 Kings 19:11–12)

God had waited five years for several reasons. In those years that I waited for God to show us this farm, the price of it went down and down. After that time, it was affordable. Before that, it would have been too expensive for us. Thank you, Lord!

25

God, Great is Thy Faithfulness!

This was taken only six months before
we moved to the mountains.

I will sing of the loving kindness of the Lord forever; To all generations I will make known Your faithfulness with my mouth. (Psalm 89:1, NASB)

The heavens will praise Your wonders, O Lord; Your faithfulness also in the assembly of the holy ones. (Psalm 89:5, NASB)

My faithfulness and My loving kindness will be with him, and in My name his horn will be exalted. (Psalm 89:24, NASB)

After writing the story "Be Still and Know that I Am God" I started meditating about what kept me going those five years in prayer? Why did I persevere in prayer when I was getting negative comments in my family, and nothing was materializing?

Then God reminded me of all the verses that He gave me as a *rhema* or a Word from Him that encouraged me through those dark days of waiting.

Here are some of those verses that kept me praying in spite of no answer. If it had not been for the Lord giving me the desire to persevere in prayer, I would have given up on that prayer, assuming that this was not of God. Let me encourage you not to give up on prayers for people or things, especially if you are not seeing an answer. God is looking for faithfulness in His children.

"The Lord preserves the *faithful*. Be strong and let your heart take courage, all you who hope in the Lord" (Psalm 31:23–24, KJV).

"A *faithful* envoy brings healing" (Proverbs 13:17b, NASB).

In Proverbs 28:20, we find "a *faithful* man shall abound with blessings" (KJV).

God talks about a *faithful* wise servant in Matthew 24:45–47.

In Matthew 25:21, God welcomes His children home with these words: "Well done, thou good and *faithful* servant; thou hast been *faithful* over a few things, I will make you ruler over many things: enter thou into the joy of the Lord" (KJV).

God is looking for *faithful* men and women who will be able to teach others (2 Timothy 2:2).

The Lord showed me several times that He was going to set my feet in a large place. Of course, I took that to mean a farm. Farms are a large place. Here are two verses that I had marked down for a promise of the farm. First, in Psalm 118:5–6, God announced to me, "From my distress I called upon the Lord; The Lord answered me and set me in a large place. The Lord is for me I will not fear." Secondly, in Psalm 31:8, God echoed, "And you have not given me over into the hand of the enemy; You have set my feet in a large place."

When I kept getting encouragement from the Lord through His Word, and my heart was stirred to keep being *faithful* to that prayer, I did not let it go by the wayside. I prayed it every day!

Even when the Lord showed us the farm, it was not smooth sailing right through until the end, and we moved immediately. No! The battle had only just begun!

Like I said yesterday, I was excited that God showed us the farm in His faithfulness on that last day, but at the same time, I was concerned that I had pushed the Lord into giving me the desire of my heart but was now going to bring leanness into my soul (Psalm 106:15).

At this time, George was extremely encouraging to me. I expressed my concern in this area, but he assured me that he was very excited about the farm and believed that it was God's will for us. He even started devising a plan to sell his veterinary practice on Hilton Head. So this gave me peace that this truly was the Lord working in our life in a mighty way!

Home we went to investigate the first step in selling our business. At first, George thought that we should try to sell it ourselves. He set the price at $250,000 for the clinic, which included several pieces of very expensive veterinary equipment, drugs, and furniture needed to operate the veterinary clinic. Also, part of the package was half an acre of land, one very large garage, two separate buildings, a pool, and by this time, a five-bedroom house, which was located above the clinic. We even had one veterinarian who came to look at it, but he did not buy it. Thank you, Lord!

After almost two months went by, our efforts were not getting us anywhere. George started making phone calls around to his friends. He found a man he had roomed with at veterinary school before we married. He had been a veterinarian for many decades but most recently had started selling medical practices for doctors. He explained that he only would consider selling one practice a year. He did not have one to sell at the moment, so he said that he would consider selling our practice. But first, he would have to come and investigate whether that would be possible. He always reserved the right to decline after he saw the contents of the practice, the building and land, and the location of our town. All these factors had to fall into place before he would consider this endeavor.

He and his wife came and spent two days calculating the value of this clinic and land. After much figuring, he agreed to sell it. His first step was to advertise in the national veterinary magazine. That advertisement was placed in the June issue. Several weeks went by with two veterinarians calling to ask questions, but neither of them even came to see the clinic. After one phone call, we never heard from them again. His selling price was six-hundred thousand dollars. Wow! If we had sold it at first, we would have practically given it away! Thank You, Lord, for saving us from giving it away!

Since the time frame was the end of May when the real estate person decided to sell it for us, I had high hopes that we would be moving by the end of the summer so as to get the children settled in only one school for that year and not two. But that did not happen. It was August before we had the best bite. This was to be the only veterinarian who came to see the clinic.

We had a phone call from a man in New Jersey in the middle of August. He made arrangements to meet with George and our real estate agent to seriously consider this clinic. When he and his family came down to look and talk, he was very interested in purchasing it. Now a date was set for the closing, October 31, 1985. We were excited that we would be able to sell it and make the move during 1985 because the capital gains tax was changing at the end of that year to our detriment.

We called the people who owned the farm and reported the good news. They were also excited. We set a date for the closure on the farm to be in November.

As the weeks progressed, I was so excited, thinking, *We will be moving and getting settled on the farm before Christmas. Wonderful!*

I was so happy and cheerful. Every day was a good day that a new life was ahead of us in a brand-new place. Especially since God had so mightily given us this farm, it was an overwhelming joy to be able to now occupy it permanently. Praise His name!

As the weeks progressed, we received a phone call in the middle of October that was discouraging beyond comprehension. It was the doctor who was to close with us the end of October that year, only two weeks away. He was asking if he could have his earnest money back so that he could buy another clinic. George, of course, said, "No!"

George had this long conversation explaining that he was to close with us in two weeks. He reneged on buying our clinic and did not seem to care that this news was very disturbing.

"Oh no! How could he do that with only two weeks to go? Now we would not be able to sell it this year to bypass the high taxes next year! God what are we going to do?" I was definitely in the pit of despair. My dream of moving to the mountains had just disappeared. "Kaput, gone forever!"

I literally cried out to the Lord and started questioning why this was happening. I was absolutely distraught. I thought that since the Lord, after five years, had so graciously answered my prayer, surely, He would at least have given us *smooth sailing* to this closing. I should have anticipated that the battle would be fierce because the enemy would fight us on this one. "Oh, well! My vision was gone, disappeared forever!" I thought.

After waiting for more than five years now, surely the Lord meant for us to possess the land. Would we be stuck there at Hilton Head forever? Would we ever get away from all the social climbing and emphasis on money? It was extremely hard raising children in such an inflated environment with an emphasis on worldly things instead of on the Lord. In some respects, it was like trying to raise children in a modern-day Sodom! We wanted our children to realize that life was not about money and pleasure; it was about being on fire for the Lord!

I fell into the depths of despair! God, how long was I going to have to wait before it would be time for us to move? Or, maybe, it never would be! Oh, God, what a death of a vision! In fact, the owners of the farm put it back on the market. They agreed that if we came up with a buyer, they would honor our agreement, but in the meantime, they would open the sale of the farm again, which was disastrously disheartening for us!

The weeks again progressed as it came up to Thanksgiving weekend. On Saturday of that weekend, we received another call from the veterinarian who had reneged on the closing. My anger raged within me as I knew that George was talking with him.

In a few minutes, George found me and said, "He wants to know if we will sell him this clinic again." My anger was getting the best of me when I said, "You tell him if he wants to buy this clinic, he will have to close by December 30 so that we can close on the farm on December 31!" I was not very nice when I said that either. If he would not be willing to do that, the sale would be off forever.

As George went back to the phone and explained this in better terms than I had, he accepted the offer and set the closing at that moment to be the exact dates that I had quoted.

So the sale once again had been renewed! My heart was wanting to be happy, but at the same time, I was being reserved just in case it did not work out again.

The weeks moved on toward Christmas. Since we had not any more negative feedback from this veterinarian, I began to consider I had better start making plans of moving out of this house by the end of the month. "What! By the end of the month?" I exclaimed to myself. "What was I going to do with Christmas upon us and the closing coming shortly thereafter?" I began to believe that maybe this time it would be complete, and we would move quickly. But would it? There was still some doubt because I felt as though I could not trust this man.

More conversations occurred, and arrangements were made so that we would not have to leave the house until the end of the first week of January 1986. Praise God! Even though he was taking over by January 1, he gave us more time to pack up. Thank You, Lord!

Christmas came, and the family enjoyed the usual Christmas with my mom. As soon as we finished unwrapping the last present, I announced that we all should start packing to move. Everyone reluctantly obeyed.

The day finally arrived for the closing of this property. As we made arrangements for the children during this procedure, we also made plans that we would leave them with my mother immediately, following this closing to travel to the mountains to finalize the ownership of our farm the next day. As soon as we all signed the papers, off we commenced to journey to our next closing before the first day of January.

Upon arriving the next morning, December 31, we found ourselves in a winter wonderland. It had not yet snowed, but the trees, roads, and people were covered with an icy haze over the whole environment. It looked as if they had had an ice storm, and the air in the day was thick with tiny ice pellets smaller than a snowflake. It was beautiful.

For someone who had been raised on the coast in the south, it was a treat. I had hoped to move to a place that would have four seasons instead of two. Lord, you are so very, very good!

When we arrived at the closing, my heart was very nervous about whether we were doing the right thing or not. When you are about to embark on a total life change when you are forty, it can be very disturbing. My heart was questioning, "Are we walking under direction of the Holy Spirit, or are we going our own way?"

Nevertheless, the closing was completed in Clayton! Immediately, we left to return to the children and my mother down on the coast. The actual date for moving had not yet been set.

When the veterinarian arrived at Hilton Head ready to start practice, they decided that we should move out right then. We had an extra small apartment in the back of the kennel where I had a preschool in the past. We converted it quickly into a living-quarters for about the last eleven days.

While we were living in that apartment with four children ranging in age from almost fifteen to almost six years old, we had a company that brought us a moving van trailer (it fit onto a semi-truck) for us to pack before leaving. This company would come and pick up the trailer and deliver it to the farm when we had it properly loaded.

We had to rid the house of all of our boxes so that the new family could move into their new house. We were very crowded with boxes and six people, one bath, and only two other rooms. Praise God from whom all blessings flow!

We packed the trailer as quickly as we could while still trying to balance the weight distribution. We went from living in a very large five-bedroom house with a den, spacious kitchen, and a humongous living room that flowed into the other living area. This house overlooked the pool and was quite comfortable. What a shock when we had at the last week to move out of our luscious house while the moving van was not yet ready.

Finally, the day came to call the moving van company about hauling that tractor trailer up to the farm. The best thing about using that trailer was we could keep it as long as we wanted. We actually kept it for six months before it was completely unloaded.

The house on the farm was undersized for our family. Its dimensions were more like a postage stamp compared to the sprawling house at Hilton Head which had five-bedrooms with generously proportioned living areas. We definitely did not have room for all of our furniture in this minute farm house.

Get this picture! There were two adults, four children, with two being teenagers and two being in elementary school, two very small bedrooms, one bath, a tiny kitchen and living area that were together. Of course, when we arrived that first night, we found out that the heater would not work well at all. In fact, we had to wake up in the night and kick the fan to keep it working. In fact, we told the children that we were all going to camp out in the living room in order to stay warm.

Also, the walls in the bedrooms were covered about halfway up with mildew. This fungus caused the walls to be black. We quickly tore out the Sheetrock and found that there was not any insolation behind it. No wonder it was especially cold back in the bedrooms.

Nevertheless, we were happy and content on our new farm that the Lord had so graciously provided. We all went discovering new things about the farm the next day after we unloaded the necessities of life. Also, it took a day or two to start the children in their new Christian school. All were excited about our new life except for our two teenagers.

Here is my mother when she visited not long after we moved.
Our bull and horse were looking for an extra treat.

26

God Will Direct Our Path

Trust in the Lord with all your heart, and lean not on your own understanding; In all your ways acknowledge Him and He will direct our paths. (Proverbs 3:5–6)

I will fear no evil; for You are with me. (Psalm 23:4b)

The Lord is my rock and my fortress and my deliverer; The God of my strength, in whom I will trust; My shield and the horn of my salvation; My stronghold and my refuge, My Savior . . . (2 Samuel 22:2–3)

His truth (Word of God) shall be your shield and buckler. (Psalm 91:4c)

Yesterday, I ended with "all were excited about our new life except for the two teenagers." All George and I could see at the time was that our older two children were being influenced by the world system more than we could imagine. That was very distressing for parents when they see their children slipping into accepting what the world demands rather than the Word of God growing stronger in their lives.

Our oldest child is a male, and he was being introduced to video games at Wal-Mart. Wal-Mart had just opened at Hilton Head, and he could walk there since it was located at that time within walking distance of our house and clinic. He spent long hours down there, filling his mind with things that were not important, especially in a spiritual sense.

Also, children raised in such a lucrative society adopt different values than their parents. Their focus is taken off the Lord and placed on material things. God verbalizes in Ephesians 2:2–5 how we are not to walk "according to the course of this world, according to the prince of the power of the air, the spirit who now works in the sons of disobedience . . . conducting ourselves in the lusts of our flesh, fulfilling the desires of the flesh and of the mind." But God would have us to be "rich in mercy, because of His great love with which He loved us, even when we were dead in trespasses, made us alive together with Christ." Thank you, Lord!

As we saw this happening in our children, we knew that something had to be done before we lose them in a spiritual sense. Their direction needed to be steered by the Word of God instead of the world.

The oldest child was almost fifteen when we moved, and the second was thirteen and a half. The first one was a basketball player for Hilton Head Christian Academy, and he loved it. He certainly was not the best player on the team, but he enjoyed learning this sport. At the time, all we could see were their spiritual needs. As he has grown older, he has shared how he was so very upset by our decision. But he certainly has grown up to love the Lord and has the right perspective on material things. The second one also loves the Lord and has her priorities straight.

Right or wrong, in their mind, God lead us to make this major move in order to steer our children in the best spiritual direction. Praise His name!

Today, I desire to share with you the actual moving day from Hilton Head to the mountains. The Lord was in every step of the way.

The first vehicle that left Hilton Head was the moving van pulled by that tractor trailer truck. He left shortly before us, and his directions were to go to the farm and leave the trailer part in a certain place. He saw where we were living at Hilton Head, and now he would see where we were going to live.

We have mentioned in earlier stories, at that time, we had a fifteen-passenger van to carry our family. We possessed one horse, Red, four dogs, three cats, and our four children. I was scheduled to drive our van while pulling the horse trailer, the four dogs were put in several compartments in the horse trailer, the cats were in the van with our four children and myself. I want to express that we were loaded to the hilt!

George was driving one of our farm trucks that was very large that we bought with the farm. We had been to the mountains, brought it back to Hilton Head in order to load the tractor that we cleared land with at Hilton Head. Also on that truck besides the tractor were many yard implements. He was packed up to his neck with equipment.

Off we went as we left Hilton Head, looking like the *Beverly Hillbillies*. George was in the lead, and I followed with my crew. He went first because he would be slower than my vehicle. We intended for him to lead the way so that we could stay together on this trip.

Every few hours, we had to stop with either the children or the pets having to use the restroom. This trip was moving at a *snail's pace* because of all the extra bodies and equipment that we were hauling.

The trip should have taken about six to seven hours at most, but with the extra load, it took all day and into the evening before we arrived in the mountains. We were traveling together most of the morning, and about middle morning, George was driving along and leading the way well until we came to a small town in South Carolina. His truck was so large that I could not see around at signs. He seemed to be not sure which way he was going, when all of a sudden, he turned to the left abruptly, and with the horse trailer, I was not prepared to do that. So away I went straight. With the heavy traffic, I was not able to turn around and follow him.

The oldest child got the map and informed me that if we continued on this path, we would meet again on the other side of Anderson, South Carolina. But in the meantime, that would not happen for several hours.

On our course, the children and I stopped several times for bathroom breaks for all of us as well as the animals. We even ate lunch that we had brought with us alongside the road at a picnic area. We were determined to make this trip enjoyable as well as pushing forward.

Many times, I kept praying for George and his load. I did not want him to turn back to look for us. "God, please allow this trip to be without mishap to vehicles, the load, or with the people," I whispered to God. Oh, and God please let us meet back up with George before we get to the mountains.

As we drove through Anderson, South Carolina, we toured the city by mistake. I had taken a wrong turn again. By this time, I was thinking, *Would I ever find George?* or *Is he broken down somewhere and needs my help?* Worry was beginning to take over my mind.

We came to a red light and had to stop. Just as I was about to be overcome by fear, I saw this truck with a colossal load in its bed. By this time, the evening shadows were falling all around us. It was hard to see for the lights of the other vehicles. As this truck passed under the stoplight, the children started yelling, "Mom, that's Daddy!" We were all so excited to see him again.

Finally, my light changed so that we could fall in right behind him. I flashed my lights to let him know it was me. He tooted back. "Thank you, God, that you reunited us before we arrived at our destination." We still had about two hours ahead of us before we arrived.

As we were pulling into our town, we spotted the truck that brought our moving trailer to the farm. We stopped and talked to him. This man said, "Why did you leave all that you had down on Hilton Head to come here? He could see the smallness of the house and the largeness of our family, and he was puzzled.

But God had other plans for us that none of us could completely comprehend at that moment. "God's eyes are on our ways" (Job 24:23b, 34:21). "His ways are not our ways; His thoughts are not our thoughts" (Isaiah 55:8–9). And in Isaiah 45:13, God reminds us "I will direct *all* his ways." We have to remember that God looks from a heavenly perspective and we can only see what is around us at that moment.

Fear has no part in the Christian's life. "There is no fear in love; but perfect love cast out fear, because fear involves torment!" (1 John 4:18). If we are loving and trusting God the way that we should, we do not have a reason to fear. Remember, Jesus will never leave us or forsake us as we think that we are walking alone in this world. He is always beside us! Many times, He is carrying us through the difficult circumstances of life (Isaiah 46:6).

He is our shield and defender (Psalm 3:3, 5:12, 33:20). Remember the fire and cloudy pillar that lead the children of Israel through their wanderings (Exodus 13:21–23), so He will lead and guide us through the circumstances of each day. In Isaiah 48:17, God instructs us, "I am the Lord your God . . . who leads you by the way you should go."

Even though Satan and his demonic cohorts are all around us as they are ruling and reigning on this earth, Jesus is the overcomer who has already won the victory for His children more than two-thousand years ago. Jesus says in John 16:33c, "I have overcome the world" (compare 1 John 5:4–5; Revelation 17:14, 3:21). Satan has been completely defeated by Jesus' blood and His sacrifice for us.

We are seated in the heavenly places with Christ Jesus even right now as we walk on this earth (Ephesians 2:6). Use the Word of God against the evil one, and he has to flee (Matthew 4:4, 7, 10).

27

God Overcomes Our Mountains

Here is George and the new tractor on a snowy
day while cleaning out chicken houses.

After arriving in the mountains, we realized that our house needed more work than we first thought. We had not gone into the house when we first saw the farm because we were not buying the house, but the land and the chicken business. At the time, I had made a comment that I was not worried about what the house looked like, because we would be building a new one quickly.

The first night that we stayed there, the heater was not working properly. This was a wall heater that had a fan in a kind of squirrel cage. After arriving on January 11, 1986 early evening, we only had opportunity to bring in a few things before retiring for the night.

Since the house was cold that January evening, we brought mattresses in the house for sleeping on the floor. We all gathered together and slept on the mattresses on the floor in a circle around the heater. Many times in the night, George had to get up and kick the squirrel cage in order to get that fan running properly again. We realized then that something else had to be done in order to stay warm.

During the first week, we purchased and installed a wood heater to warm the house. That was the only economical type of heat that we were able to afford at that time. We had 125 acres of land that had many acres of forest all around us. We had an unending supply of wood for the fire place. George installed that within a short time for us to be warm that cold snowy winter.

Our house had another problem that was very evident as soon as we walked into it. The walls in the bedrooms were black with mold about half way from the floor to the ceiling. The Sheetrock had to be torn out and replaced. Upon tearing that out, we realized that there was not any insulation in those walls.

Furthermore, this house was built in the earlier 1900's so the wiring was old. In our church that we had joined within the first few weeks of arriving, we became friends with Bill and LeAnn. Their first child was about the same age as our youngest child. Bill was an electrical engineer, so he helped George replace all the wiring in the entire house.

After completing adding insulation in the walls, rewiring, and replacing Sheetrock, we redecorated the inside of the house. The wall between the kitchen and the living area was torn out to make one larger room so that we would have more space for us to maneuver. New carpet and vinyl were placed on the floors and all the walls were repainted to freshen this old house. These projects took several months to be completed.

At the same time, we were having to get the chicken houses ready for new baby chicks. The former owner overlapped with his last grow of chickens a few weeks after we arrived, but then it was our responsibility to take over. While redecorating the house, we were readying 8 chicken houses for occupancy of new baby chicks. This was a mammoth job.

It was major house cleaning in the chicken houses as well as our house. The chicken houses had to be blown out with a blower machine and the manure from the previous grow had to be removed with the tractor before the new baby chicks could be placed in it. Also, all the drinkers and the trays for food for baby chicks had to be washed by hand with a hose. Many days and evenings we were out in the blowing snow readying these houses.

Another problem that cropped up was the lack of the proper tractor to do the work in those houses. We had bought the equipment that went with the farm in the original purchase, but the tractor was very old and it had major problems. After trying to fix it many times within in the first few weeks, we decided that we needed to trade it in so that we could get a newer model so the repairs would not be so great. When we went to the tractor dealership and traded in our old tractor for a new one, the salesman sold us a tractor that was not prepared to meet the challenges that we needed in the chicken house. In fact, our neighbor came by and asked our oldest son who was trying to clean out one of those houses, "Who sold you that *Tonka Toy?*" The neighbor explained that the tractor dealer should have known better than to sell us the tractor that was too light-weight for this job.

After relating this information to the dealership, we started searching for a larger tractor, but less expensive than a new one. We were able to find a used tractor that was priced at fifteen instead of the twenty-two thousand. We went back to the dealership and told them what we had found. To keep from losing the sale, the dealership offered to sell us a new larger tractor for the price of the used one. He knocked off seven-thousand dollars. Wow! Praise God!

While all of these repairs to equipment and the house had to be made, we had given all of our financial information to the accountant to prepare our taxes for the year that we sold the veterinary clinic and bought the farm. We established ourselves with the accountant who had been doing the books for the farm before we bought it. We were excited that he knew about the farm and would be our best choice.

In April, he contacted us when he was complete with his final figure for what we owed the government the previous year when we sold the veterinary practice. He announced to us that we owed thirty-five thousand dollars to the federal government. We just about had a "heart attack" over that figure. We asked if there was any refiguring that could be done to reduce it. "No!" he said. He seemed to not have any compassion for this problem. He was very dogmatic that he was right and we had no recourse. This would ruin us financially!, we commented

After paying him for the work that he had already done, we contacted our pastor to investigate if he knew someone who could help us. We needed a bookkeeper that was on the *cutting edge* in accounting. He immediately gave us the name of a woman from his hometown, who was only two hours away.

Straightway, we contacted her, and she agreed to look into the matter. We met her in person and went over the figures. George made some suggestions himself that she was able to implement along with her vast knowledge of accounting. Several weeks later, she communicated to us that she had reduced those taxes down to twelve thousand dollars. Praise God! That was still a lot of money, but not nearly as high as it was.

At that time, she explained to us the fact that we could also apply for a refund from several back years using income averaging. This, in the long run, would get us twelve-thousand dollars in tax refunds over the next six months. Consequently, we prepared to file those taxes with her figures.

How were we going to round up the *twelve-thousand dollars* that needed to be sent in with the taxes? Our finances were very much strained as the buyer at Hilton Head could not give us forty-thousand dollars at the time of the sale of the veterinary clinic that we had requested. By this time, we were down to being broke. As we considered what could our options be, God reminded us that we had bought the brand new larger tractor within a few weeks of moving here. This could be mortgaged so that we would be able to get a bank loan. Praise God that You went before us and led us to buy that new tractor instead of the cheaper used one. We would not have been able to mortgage the used one for anything. Thank you, God!

With the money that the bank loaned us, we filed our taxes with payment. After six months, we began to receive tax refund checks. After receiving several of these refund checks from various years in the past, we then were able to pay the bank the twelve thousand dollars back. Thank You, God!

That was truly a mammoth problem that God lifted from us! We praised God for showing our accountant how to legally restructure those taxes. That was truly a gift from Him!

Have you ever felt as though your troubles were so great and mounting higher each day that you would not be able to rise above them? I would have to say that I felt just that way. How would we be able to rise above these financial troubles?

God made it plain that if we were to overcome our mountain of troubles, we would have to completely "cast our cares on Him" (1 Peter 5:7). God reminded us that He feeds even the smallest sparrow, and we are more valuable than many sparrows (Matthew 10:29-31). Furthermore, God says, "if God makes the lilies to be much more glorious than Solomon in all of his glory and He clothes the grass of the field that is here today and gone tomorrow, how much more will He clothe us, O Ye of little faith?" (Luke 12:27-28)

Certainly, this was a faith builder! (Romans 10:17) Overcoming obstacles that were truly mightier that we are can only be done by studying God's Word and completely casting ourselves on Him. In 1 Peter 5:6-10 gives us the advice for life in all of its glory when it is about to swallow us up in an ocean of problems.

"Humble yourselves under the mighty hand of God, that He may exalt you in due time, casting all your care upon Him, for He cares for You. Be sober, be vigilant; because your adversary the devil walks about like a roaring lion, seeking whom he may devour. Resist him, steadfastly in the faith, knowing that the same sufferings are experienced by your brotherhood in the world. But may the God of all grace who called us to His eternal glory by Christ Jesus, after you have suffered a while, perfect, establish, strengthen, and settle you." (Cf. 1 Corinthians 1:9)

Certainly, this was a faith builder! Let us now discover how we will have faith to overcome the world.

28

Be on Fire for God!

As D. L. Moody once said in his book, <u>*The Secret Power*</u>, "I would rather die than live as I once did, a mere nominal Christian, and not used by God in building up His kingdom. It seems a poor empty life to live for the sake of self. Let us seek to be vessels meet for the Master's use!"

Today, we see the church at large as being liberal and superficial. Most Christians seem not to have a reverend regard for the Word of God. They seem to be living in the confines of the church a life that is not reaching out to others with an evangelistic heart. The church at large seems to be like the Laodiceans in Revelation 3:14-22. God told them "they were neither cold nor hot . . . So, then, because you are lukewarm . . . I will vomit you out of my mouth." (v. 15-16)

John MacArthur states in his commentary of Revelation 3:14-19 that the Laodiceans had an extremely serious heresy in this church. They believed that "Jesus Christ was a created being (cf. Colossians 1:15-20). Instead, He is the 'Beginning' (literally 'beginner, origina-tor, initiator') of creation (cf. John 1:3, 3:14) and the 'firstborn of creation'; that is, the most preeminent, supreme person ever born (Colossians 1:15). As a man, He had a beginning, but as God, He was the beginning. Sadly, this heresy concerning the person of Christ had produced an unregenerate church.

Because of this, that church was neither cold, openly rejecting Christ, nor hot, filled with spiritual zeal. Instead, its members were lukewarm, hypocrites professing to know Christ, but not truly belonging to Him (cf. Matthew 7:21-23). These self-deceived hypocrites sickened Christ." They "said" they knew Him, but their lives were not filled with spiritual fruit that would testify of this truth (Matthew 7:16, 19-20; John 15:2, 4-8, 16).

In verses 17-19, God paints a picture of where most people in the church are today. "Because you say, I am rich, have become wealthy, and have need of nothing—and do not know that you are wretched, miserable, poor, blind, and naked—I counsel you to buy from Me gold refined in the fire, that you may be rich; and white garments, that you may be clothed, that the shame of your nakedness may not be revealed; and anoint your eyes with eye salve, that you may see. As many as I love, I rebuke and chasten. Therefore, be zealous and repent!"

I believe that a lot of so called "Christians" today fall into the lukewarm category. They are sitting on the fence between the church and the world wondering which way to go, believing that Jesus was only a good man or a prophet. They are constantly vacillating in their commitment to the Lord as were the Laodiceans.

Jesus goes on to give everyone the same invitation. "Behold I stand at the door and knock. If anyone hears My voice and opens the door, I will come into him, and dine with him, and he with Me. To him who *overcomes*, I will grant to sit with Me (Jesus) on My throne, as I also *overcame* and sat down with My Father on His throne. He who has an ear, let him hear what the Spirit says to the churches." Revelation 3:20-22

This Laodicean Church bore Christ's name, but did not have any true believers in it. If one member would have recognized his or her spiritual bankruptcy and would have responded in genuine faith, Christ would have entered the church. (Rev. 3:20)

After responding to God in genuine repentance, God means for His children to build their faith in Him. Building faith in God comes by learning and discovering His Word to show us what a mighty God we have and seeing that same God working mightily in our own lives to help us. Any true believer in Jesus that gives themselves as a daily *living sacrifice* to the Lord to be used in whatever way God chooses is an *overcomer in Jesus!* Our faith must grow in the Lord for us to wholly trust God. "For whatever is born of God *overcomes* the world. And this is the victory that has *overcome* the world—our faith". (1 John 5:4-5)

There are three characteristics to be an overcomer as stated in John MacArthur's Study Bible, page 1972. This comes from 1 John 5:1-5. Mr. MacArthur gives these as characteristics of an over-comer—*saving faith, love,* and *obedience.* After meditating on his outline, this is what God gave me to expound on his thoughts. The fourth characteristic is based in Revelation 12:11 and other thoughts that God revealed:

Overcomers must have:

I. *Right thinking about God and who Jesus is.* We must know who Jesus truly is and what He has done (1 John 5:1) as set forth in His Word.

    a) Jesus is the *Christ.* He is the *Messiah,* God's *anointed One.* In Isaiah 9:6 He is called the *Mighty God.* He is the Savior and Lord of all mankind. Jesus, even though He knew no sin, nailed our sins to His cross and died with the wrath or anger of God on Him so that we would not have to bear our deserved punishment for our own sins (Romans 6:4-14; John 3:1-18; 1Peter 2:24; 1 John 5:11-13).

    b) Jesus is the *Word of God* from eternity past and the foun-dation of the world (John 1:1-3, 14; cf. Genesis 1). MacArthur's Study Bible, pg. 1573, states "God's Word (Jesus) is His powerful self-expression in *creation, wisdom, revelation, and salvation.*"

      In *creation* God, translated from Elohim, is a plural word. God states in Genesis 1:26 "Let *Us* make man in *Our* likeness" (Cf. Psalm 33:6-9; Job 26:7-14). This plu-rality helps us understand that God, the Father, the Son, and the Holy Spirit are One that were at creation (Cf. Isaiah 40:28-29; 45:8, 12-13, 18; 48:13; Acts 17:24-28).

In the New Testament, God spoke through His Son, the Word of God, as the creator of the world (John 1:3; Hebrews 1:2b). Jesus was created as a man at a point in time, but He was in eternity past as Elohim (Cf. John 10:30, 37-38; 14:11).

God reveals Himself in *wisdom* in Isaiah 11:2; Proverbs 8:22-31, 33-36; Psalm 104:24. This wisdom is shown to be found in Jesus in Colossians 2:2d-3; 1 Corinthians 1:21-24, 30.

In Galatians 1:12, Revelation 1:1, Ephesians 3:3-7, Hebrews 1:2a, we see that God *revealed* Himself in the man named Jesus.

Since Jesus is the Messiah, *salvation* was brought to mankind" (2 Corinthians 5:17-21; Romans 1:16-17; Acts 4:10-12; Psalm 3:8). Jesus willingly laid down His perfect life for our sinful life at the Cross of Calvary to become our Savior from sin (Matthew 1:18-21; Hebrews 10:9-10, 12, 14, 17-23).

c) Jesus is the *fullness of the Godhead bodily* (Colossians 1:19-20; 2:9). He has the fullness of the divine nature (cf. Ephesians 3:16-19; 1 Corinthians 2:9-12). He was 100% God and 100% man at the same time. He met Satan in Matthew 4 as a man and at the cross bore our sins as the perfect second Adam, but He was able to show the world the fullness of who God really was, is, and is to come.

d) Jesus is *The Great I Am* (Exodus 3:14; John 8:28-29, 37-38, cf. Revelation 1:8). Even as Moses met the Great I Am in Exodus, we meet with The Great I Am when we come to know Jesus. Jesus gives us many *I AM* statements in John:

1. *I Am* the bread that came down from heaven (John 6:41; compare Exodus 16:31-35). When Jesus made this statement, He was declaring that He was equal with the Father. *I AM* the bread of life (John 6:47-

51, 53-58). Jesus explains these statements in verse 51. "*I AM* the living bread which came down from heaven. If anyone eats of this bread, he will live forever; and the bread that I shall give is My flesh, which I shall give for the life of the world." (Cf. John 3:13-18; 7:28b-29; Hebrews 10:5-10; Psalm 40:6-8).

2. *I AM* the light of the world (John 8:12; 9:5; 1:4-5; 12:45-46). In the Old Testament, the time of Messiah would be an age when He would shine light for His people (Psalm 27:1; 119:105; Malachi 4:2; cf. Exodus 13:21-22; 14:19-25; Habakkuk 3:4; Isaiah 60:19-20; cf. Revelation 21:23-24).

3. *I AM* the door (John 10:7, 9-10; cf. 14:6). Jesus portrays Himself as the gate or only way of salvation. There is no spiritual security apart from Him (Acts 4:12; Matthew 7:13-14). By Jesus declaring that He is the door, He is claiming to be the Messiah, Son of God, and the only way of being saved (2 Timothy 1:8-10, 12; cf. 2:19).

4. *I AM* the good shepherd (John 10:11, 14-18; Psalm 23; Isaiah 40:11). As the good shepherd, Jesus declares that He will give His life for His sheep. This is reference to Him as our Savior who gave His life for us on the Cross. He nailed our sin to His cross and died in our place so that we will have life evermore (John 10:15; cf. 15:13; Colossians 2:11-15; Hebrews 9:24-28; 10:9-10, 12-25).

Not only do we have a *good shepherd,* but God has made Jesus our *Great Shepherd.* In Hebrews 13:20-21 God shows us our great shepherd. "Now may the God of peace who brought up our Lord Jesus from the dead, that great Shepherd of the sheep, through the blood of the everlasting covenant, make you complete in every good work to do His will, working in you what is well pleasing in His sight, through Jesus Christ, to whom be glory forever and ever. Amen." (cf. Romans 5:1, 2, 10)

5. *I AM* the Son of God (John 10:36-38; Matthew 3:13-17; 4:6; 17:5; Romans 1:3-4; 5:10; 8:3, 29, 32; cf. Galatians 2:20; 4:4, 6; Hebrews 1:2-5). The Son, who is our high priest (Hebrews 7:26-28), is the second person of the Godhead. He, at a point in time, came to this earth to show the world the Father and to die for our sins so that we would have eternal life (John 3:16-17; cf. Luke 9:56). God the Father affirmed Jesus as His Son at His baptism (Matthew 3:13-17; Mark 1:9-11; Luke 3:21-23), His transfiguration (Matthew 17:1-13; cf. 2 Peter 1:16-18), and through His resurrection (1 Peter 1:3-5; 1 Corinthians 15:13-28).

6. *I AM* the resurrection and the life (John 11:25-26; 5:21, 29; cf. Philippians 3:10-11; Romans 1:3-6; 6:5). Because Jesus was raised from the dead by the power of the Father, so we are raised to life in Jesus (1Corinthians 15:12-28). Because Jesus was raised from the dead, we have a living hope (1Peter 1:3-5)

7. *I AM* the way, the truth, and the life. No man comes to the Father but by Me (John 14:6-11; 3:15; 10:38; 11:25). Grace and truth came by Jesus Christ (John 1:17). "The Word became flesh and dwelt among us, and we beheld His glory, the glory as of the only begotten of the Father, full of grace and truth" (v. 14). The truth will set you free (John 8:32)

8. *I AM* the *true vine* (John 15:1, 5) and My Father is the caretaker (v. 1). There are 2 types of branches coming out of the vine—fruitful (vv. 2, 8), and non-fruitful (vv. 2, 6). The branches that bear fruit are the true believers; the ones that do not bear fruit are not true Christians. They are counterfeit (Matthew 7:13-23).

Not only is the fruitful vine evidence of salvation, but the true believer must abide in Jesus. Abiding means to stay with or remain in contact. We need to stay close to Jesus and His Words need to be in us by memorizing and meditating on them (John 15:7; 8:31; Colossians 1:23; Hebrews 3:4-6; 2 Timothy 3:14-17; cf. Romans 11:19-23).

II. *Love God and others* (1 John 5:1b-3a). D.L. Moody says in his book *The Secret Power*, "Love for people is the first evidence of our love for God (1 John 3:11, 16, 18, 23). When love is triumphant in our heart, true joy is the result; peace is love in repose; and long suffering is love on trial (1 Peter 3:18).

When we are full of the love of God, we are, then, compelled to work for God, and God blesses. Love is God's crown and the dome of all graces. Love is a mighty ocean in its greatness, dwelling with and flowing from the Eternal Spirit. We must be compelled by the love of Christ (2 Corinthians 5:14-15). God's love must burn so deeply in our heart, spirit, and mind that we cannot sit idly by and be silent while others are going to hell (Ephesians 3:19).

If we have an unforgiving spirit toward anyone, we are not abiding in God and His love. Unforgiveness equals a lack of love for God and others. We are not qualified to work for God with a root of bitterness in our heart. Love and forgiveness are essential elements for spiritual power."

God deserves that we love Him with our whole-heart (Mark 12:30-31; Hebrews 10:22 (true heart). In Joshua 14:8-9, 14, Joshua and Caleb *wholly* followed God (Numbers 32:12).

God instructs us in 1 John 4:7-8, 12, 20-21 "Beloved, let us love one another, for love is of God; and everyone who loves is born of God and knows God. He who does not love does not know God, for God is love . . . If we love one another, God abides in us, and His love has been perfected in us . . . If anyone says, 'I love God,' and hates his brother, he is a liar; for he who does not love his brother who he has seen, how can he love God whom he has not seen? And this commandment we have from Him: that he who loves God must love his brother also." Furthermore, in 1 Peter 1:22 we are told "Since you have purified your souls in obeying the truth through the Spirit in sincere love of the brethren, love one another fervently with a pure heart." (1 John 3:16-23).

In fact, we are to love our enemies (Matthew 5:44; Luke 6:27-36). We, also, are not to judge or condemn, but forgive and give to our enemies (v. 37-38; Matthew 6:12, 14-15; 18:28-35). In Psalm 145:8-9 David tells us "The Lord is gracious and full of compassion, slow to anger and great in mercy. The Lord is good to all, and His tender mercies are over all His works."

As the Lord is full of compassion, so we should extend compassion to our enemies also. As Jesus was dying on the cross, He said "Father, forgive them for they do not know what they do (Luke 23:34). Likewise, we must show a sincere, goodwill toward our enemies.

III. *Have obedience to God's commands* (1 John 5:2b-3; Jeremiah 7:23; Acts 5:29; Romans 6:16; Hebrews 5:9; cf. 1 Peter 4: 16-19). Obedience brings blessings. The entire Bible is full of blessing and cursing. It starts in the Old Testament in Genesis 12 through Revelation 7 (cf. Deuteronomy 11:26-28). "A faithful man will abound with blessings" (Proverbs 28:20; cf. 10:6; 1 Peter 3:9-12).

In John 14:21 we find that obedience to God's commands shows that we love God, and God will disclose Himself to those who obey His Word. Everyone who verbalizes "I know Jesus" must meditate on these Scriptures. In 1 John 2:4-11, God affirms these thoughts: a) "He who says, 'I know Him' and does not keep His commandments is a liar, and the truth is not in him (v. 4); b) He who abides in Him ought himself also to walk just as He (Jesus) walked (v. 6); c) He who says he is in the light and hates his brother, is in darkness until now (v. 10)." MacArthur says, "True believers are to abide in Jesus (John 15:1-6) which means they, walk in truth (2 John 4:3; 3 John 4), and persevere in faithfulness (3 John 5; Matthew 24:45-46) and sound doctrine" (2 Timothy 3:16; Titus 2; cf. Ephesians 4:14).

Saying we know Him and *truly* knowing Him are two different things. Jesus must say that He knows you. Many "so called" Christians will be shocked and dismayed when Jesus says "I never knew you" (Matthew 7:231-23). Having a personal relationship with Jesus as your *Savior/Master* and obedience to His Word is the key to whether you truly know Him and He knows you.

IV. *Walk in the power of the Holy Spirit* (Romans 8:14).

When we are walking in the power of the Holy Spirit, we will become *overcomers* for Jesus. *Overcomers* cannot have sin reigning in their life (Romans 6:12). They will recognize when they sin and ask, immediately, to be forgiven. Furthermore, they will have a victorious ministry against Satan by plucking souls from the fires of hell.

In Revelation 12:11 God tells us how we can overcome Satan in this life. "And they *overcame* him by the blood of the Lamb and by the word of their testimony, and they did not love their lives to the death."

The *blood of the Lamb* protects us from the wiles of Satan. Nothing can stand against us when we belong to Jesus, not even Satan and his friends (Romans 8:31-39).

The word of our testimony is when we tell others what God has done for us. We are to tell how God has forgiven us and how we see the hand of God in our lives.

They did not love their lives means that they loved God more than they loved living on earth. They were willing to give up their life for the sake of others in order to glorify God. God must be completely number one in their life.

How do we *walk in the Spirit?* Walking in the Spirit in a nutshell is trusting, delighting, committing, resting, and waiting for the Lord (Psalm 37:3-7; 40:8; 119:16, 47; cf. Romans 7:22), seeking God's face (Psalm 27:4, 8, 14), being still to hear His voice (Psalm 46:10; cf. Habakkuk 2:1; Jeremiah 33:3), and giving your life as a living sacrifice to His service (Romans 12:2).

a) Diligently *seek the face of God* every day. In prayer enter into close communion with God. Ask God to speak to you through His Word. God will give us a *word* from Him that is especially for you. That is called a *rhema*. It can be an answer to prayer, your marching orders for that day, or what He has for you in the future. *Rhemas* are verses that seem to *slap you in the face*. They will mean a great deal to you or you will realize their worth as the days unfold.

Pray this prayer in Colossians 1:9-14 every day. Ask God to show you "that you may be filled with the knowledge of His will in all wisdom and spiritual understanding; that you may walk worthy of the Lord, fully pleasing Him, being fruitful in every good work and increasing in the knowledge of God; strengthened with all might, according to His glorious power, for all patience and longsuffering with joy; giving thanks to the Father who has qualified us to be partakers of the inheritance of the saints in the light . . . "

Purify your soul by allowing the Word of God to cleanse you. (John 15:3; 17:17; 1 John 1:7, 9; 3 John 11). Your soul is your mind, will, and emotions—your personality. When we are *born again* (John 3), our spirit is renewed by the Holy Spirit who takes up residence there, but our soul contains the filthiness of the world. Our souls need to be purified from the presence of sin. Ask forgiveness of your daily sins. Keep a short account!

b) *Praise and worship* God before you start to pray for your requests. Tell God how much He means to you and memorize Bible verses that tell who He is and what He has done for you. Show Him His worth before you give your requests.

c) Be a *living sacrifice* to God. "Present your body as a living sacrifice, holy, acceptable to God, which is your reasonable service. And do not be conformed to this world, but be transformed by the renewing of your mind, that you may prove what is that good and acceptable and perfect will of God." (Romans 12:1-2). We all must be walking in the fruit of the Spirit daily (Galatians 5:22-25). These verses are not a suggestion to live by, but a command!

d) *Abide in Christ* (John 15). Genuine salvation will cause you to remain in and live for God. If you abide in the Word of God (the Bible), you will be Jesus' disciples (John 8:31). Also, "If you abide in Me, and My words abide in you, you will ask what you desire, and it shall be done for you" (John 15:7). This does not mean that we can ask selfishly and obtain what we want. MacArthur states in his commentary on John 15:7-10, "true believers obey the Lord's commands, submitting to His Word (John 14:21, 23). Because of their commitment to God's Word, they are devoted to His will, thus their prayers are fruitful (John 14:13-14), which puts God's glory on display as He answers."

If we are abiding, we will desire to win souls for His glory. Luke 4:18 is our commission, as Christians, while on earth—"preach the gospel to the poor, heal the broken hearted, proclaim liberty to the captives, and recovery of sight to the blind, to set at liberty those who are oppressed, and to proclaim the acceptable year of the Lord."

God means for us to "bear much fruit" (John 15:5, 16). Fruit can be godly attitudes as stated in Galatians 5:22, righteous behavior (Philippians 1:11), and leading others to faith in Jesus (Romans 1:16). We must possess all of these types of fruit for us to be effective witnesses for God" (MacArthur).

We do not need to witness to everyone who passes us on the street, but find *people of faith.* How do you find these people? Whenever you are talking with someone, ask them if you can pray for them. One example would be a server in a restaurant. *People of faith* would be willing for you to bless them and pray for them. If they allow this, share the gospel with them either by giving it verbally or using your personal tract that you create. Some will even pray right then to receive Jesus. If the circumstance does not allow for that, pray for them regularly in prayer time.

Recently, I was in a store and the cashier was particularly friendly. As we talked while checking out, the Holy Spirit encouraged me to give her one of our family tracts that we write and have printed. It has a funny picture of our entire family on the front.

As she viewed this picture, she started to laugh. I said, "Read it when you get home". She answered loudly as I was leaving, "I will read it!"

Two of my recent divine appointments were located at the mouth of our driveway. It is a very isolated spot with practically no traffic in this area. The first was someone that had recently moved to our road. We spent many months together as this person went to several Bible studies with me.

Another was a person that had lost her way and was, in fact, far away from where her friend had instructed her to come. With this one, we talked for more than an hour and we got to know each other. I was able to share several stories of my life that showed God's hand working mightily on my behalf. I was able to present the gospel with her and give one of our family tracts.

The third one had gotten my phone number off the computer that was listed seven years prior by our son with his advertisement. We became connected with each other as she had a love for goat's milk. These were three of my best opportunities to share Christ lately. I pray for all of these people often.

I believe that God will give us a divine appointment to talk with these kinds of people when you are least expecting it. Be sensitive to the leading of the Holy Spirit. God knows who is seeking Him and who is not. Be bold and don't miss an opportunity.

e) *Expectantly listen for God's voice* to speak to you. God speaks to us through *His Word.* God speaks in Hebrews

4:12 through our *"thoughts and intents of the heart,"* a *"still small voice"* (1 Kings 19:11-12), and *circumstances of life.* Job 33:14-19 says "For God may speak in one way or another, yet man does not perceive it. In a *dream*, in a *vision* of the night . . . *He opens the ears* of men . . . Man is chastened *by pain*."

Furthermore, Jesus in Revelation 3:20 says "I stand at the door and knock. If anyone *hears My voice* and opens the door, I will come into him." (Cf. Hebrews 12:24-25) Jesus is seeking intimacy with believers, so He knocks and speaks to them.

In my life's verse, God says "Call unto me and *I will answer* you, and show you great and mighty things which you do not know." (Jeremiah 33:3) God assures us that when we seek Him in prayer, He will answer us, so we need to listen carefully for His answer. It will come.

Isaiah 45:3 says God will call us by name. God called the boy, Samuel, in 1 Samuel 3 and he answered God by saying "Speak, Lord, your servant hears." (v.9b) Here God used His *still small voice* to speak to Samuel.

When you *hear* His voice speaking to you, check out what you heard through His Word to prove its accuracy. After checking it out in the Word, ask God to confirm it through Christian mentors or circumstances of life. Moreover, God will confirm His Word through giving you peace in your heart (Philippians 4:7; John 14:27; cf. Romans 8:6; 15:13; Galatians 5:22; Ephesians 2:14).

Jesus expects an *overcomer* to boldly go into the enemy's territory and snatch God's smoking flax (Isaiah 42:3; Matthew 12:20) from the eternal fires of hell. This term was used to help people who know Jesus to find those who do not have a relationship with Him as yet and bring them into a saving relationship. We, as Christians, need to have tender compassion for them as Christ did. We need to boldly snatch them from the clutches of Satan.

Jesus expects Christians to know who they are in Christ and to remember that we are seated in heavenly places in Christ. Since the devil is under Jesus' feet, he is under the true Christian's feet also (Ephesians 1:19-22; cf. 6:10-19). We are more than conquerors through Him who loved us (Romans 8:38-39). We need to tread confidently and shamelessly into Satan's territory to claim souls for Jesus!

Here are other Scriptures that teach us about *overcomers*—Revelation 2:7, 11, 17, 26-28; 3:5, 12, 21.

Know the Word, and apply it to your problems, and you will *overcome* the evil one. For that is how Jesus *overcame* him in Matthew 4!

29

God Is Always Watching and Protecting

This picture was taken the same time that
Bill was helping George in this story.

For affliction does not come from the dust, nor does trouble come from the ground; Yet man is born to trouble, as the sparks fly upward. (Job 5:6–7, NKJV)

Whoever listens to Me will dwell safely, and will be secure without fear of evil. (Proverbs 1:33, NKJV)

It was still winter in the mountains of 1986. We had only been in residence in our new farm for about two months. Our older children wanted to go back to Hilton Head for a visit, and also, I had an appointment with my dentist who had started work on my teeth that was not quite complete.

So off to Hilton Head I went with three of our 4 children. David wanted to stay on the farm with his dad. We took our flight in the morning of Friday. We arrived just in time for my appointment. When that was complete, we had the rest of the weekend to play and enjoy.

Since the children and I were gone for the weekend, George invited his friend, Bill, over to help him do some electrical work. Bill was an electrical engineer who loved to help others, especially when they had just moved to town. (Oh, by the way, Bill's wife, LeAnn, was the woman in the story about coming to look for the farm, who was not friendly. She sat in the rocking chair on the front porch of her friend's house and would not say a word that very first day we met her. She was the one who was wondering if we were the ax murderers!) But at this time, she was truly my best friend.

Back to the story. George and Bill were dangerous when they got together. There was no telling what they would get into. As I mentioned in another story already, we had bought the new Tonka Toy tractor, and it had a backhoe on the rear end of it.

It was Saturday morning when Bill arrived to work with George. Work commenced about seven o'clock in the morning. They had various projects on their agenda.

Seeing that Bill was an electrical engineer as his occupation, he volunteered to help George rewire our very small house. Not only did we need to tear out the existing Sheetrock because of the black mildew that were growing so nicely on it from the floor to about half way up the wall, but also, they had decided that the Sheetrock had to come out. It was a perfect opportunity to rewire the house that was built in the 1950s.

After working all through the morning and afternoon rewiring, they decided to embark on a water problem. We were having trouble with water getting in the basement. One of the water pipes was leaking in the backyard, draining down into the basement. And, of course, since the small tractor that we had not yet taken back had a backhoe on it, George was trying to accomplish this project before Monday when he had to return it to the dealer because it was not big enough. Also, since it was George's favorite play toy, Bill had to try it out along with George.

As they were digging around with the backhoe in the yard looking for the leak, all of a sudden, Bill was driving the tractor when it appeared that Mount Vesuvius had erupted! Sparks and lightning bolts flashed through the air in the backyard as they hit the electric cable that supplied the pond shed with power. They reported later that it was quite a show of deadly dynamite. Additionally, an electric breaker in the house flipped causing power to cease. About that time, David came to the front door reporting that the power had gone off in the house.

The problem was as they backed the tractor off the electric line, they hit a water main. Water now began bursting forth like the "old faithful geyser" in Yellowstone National Park. Now they had double-trouble because snow and ice lay all over the ground and the roads. They were going to have to travel up the mountain quite a distance to turn this water off. It was on the hillside up a gravel dirt road, but ice covered the road so much that they were not able to walk or drive a vehicle there. They had to use the four-wheel drive tractor to pull off this feat.

While they were progressing up this slippery roadway on the side of the mountain, about five or six thousand gallons of water began discharging from the tank all over the backyard into the night air. What a sloppy, muddy mess on top of the ice layer that already lay on the ground!

What other disasters could these two men instigate next! There seemed to be misfortune ready to happen all around them that night. It appeared as though they were two little boys looking for mischief. The only difference between men and boys is the size of their toys!

When LeAnn and I heard about it, we decided that they should not be allowed to "play" together anymore without additional supervision. Seriously, we were very thankful that both of them were still alive after that day and evening together.

I am so thankful that we, as God's children, are invincible until He is finished with us. "For the eyes of the Lord run to and fro throughout the whole earth, to show Himself strong on behalf of those whose heart is loyal to Him" (2 Chronicles 16:9).

God is looking for obedience from His children. Jesus said, "If you love Me, Keep My Commandments (John 14:15). Obedience to His commands doesn't save us, but obedience shows that we have love for Jesus. We should want to obey because He suffered and died for our sins. He exchanged or imputed His perfect life for our sinful life so that we might have eternal life in Him forever.

Hope, love, obedience, and faith are all intertwined together so that you cannot separate one from the other. They are meshed together inseparably so it is hard to decide which one would come first. Some may argue that faith would have to come first, but others may say that hope would be the spark. I would like to imagine that hope would be the first ember of life in coming to know Jesus. God plants a desire in us all by the Holy Spirit for us to want to know God. As this desire grows and is fed by knowledge of God's Word, our faith will increase. Love is born from knowing and believing the truth about God and what He has done for us. Out of love, obedience sprouts. We will obey those that we love and trust. These four concepts, no matter which one comes in the beginning, are all born when God pursues each one of us to know Him.

In 2 Corinthians 1:20-22 we see that first God, through Jesus Christ, calls us to Himself before we even are aware of what is taking place in life. He, then, anoints us when we respond to accepting Jesus as our Lord and Savior. By His Spirit, we are sealed "until the day of redemption" (1 Peter 1:3-5). Next, we are given His Spirit in our hearts as a down payment for what is to come (Ephesians 1:13-14, 19; cf. 2:4-10; 2 Timothy 1:8-12). Our desire for God starts and ends with Him (John 6:44; cf. John 17:1-2, 11, 20-22).

1. Hope is the absolute assurance of future eternal life that is to come. We can be sure of our hope because the "same power that raised Jesus from the dead" (1 Peter 1:3–5) is the same power that keeps us saved when we truly come to know Him. We are "sealed with the Holy Spirit of promise who is the guarantee of our inheritance until the redemption of the purchased possession, to the praise of His glory" (Ephesians 1:13c–14).

The Holy Spirit is given to true believers at the time of salvation, pledging that in the future time, we are guaranteed of our eternal inheritance. In John 10:28–29, Jesus said,

I give them eternal life, and they shall never perish; neither shall any man snatch them out of My Father's Hand. My Father, who has given them to Me is greater than all; and no one is able to snatch them out of My Father's Hand.

Our hope is a living hope based on Jesus' resurrection from the dead (1 Peter 1:3). It is an "inheritance that is incorruptible and undefiled and that does not fade away reserved in Heaven for you, who are kept by the power of God *through faith* for salvation ready to be revealed in the last time" (1 Peter 1:3–5).

2. Love is giving! Jesus provided salvation for all mankind, but we have to receive it to claim it (John 1:12). Jesus opened His arms wide to receive the whole earth if they would but look to Him for salvation.

God loves all people and desires that "all should come to repentance" (2 Peter 3:9). He loved us so much that He was willing to give His only Son to die for our sins. There is not a greater love than that.

We should love God and others. Others should be a priority above ourselves, but not above God.

3.   Obedience does not secure salvation for anyone, but it shows that you love God. It is linked with rewards in heaven (1 Corinthians 3:11-15), as well as God manifesting Himself to us in life on earth (John 14:21). If we are doing what God chooses for us, we will be rewarded for our faithfulness to those tasks.

4.   Faith comes by hearing, learning, and studying the Word of God (Romans 10:17, cf. 1:17, 3:21–28; 5:1–2; 9:30). That is why we need to study, learn, memorize, and meditate on His Word. Faith is the "victory that overcomes the world" (1 John 5:4b). God supplies us a "shield of faith to quench all the fiery darts of the wicked one" (Ephesians 6:16). Our salvation is based on faith in Jesus Christ.
      Faith in God is at the basis of all our lives:

      a)   Salvation is by faith (Ephesians 2:8-10).
      b)   We are justified by faith (Romans 5:1).
      c)   We live by faith (Romans 1:17).
      d)   Our hearts are purified by faith (Acts 15:9).
      e)   We are sanctified by faith (Acts 26:18).
      f)   We have obedience to the faith (Romans 1:5; 2 Corinthians 10:5; cf. 1 Corinthians 16:13).
      g)   We are kept by the power of God through faith (1 Peter 1:5).
      h)   We are healed by faith (Isaiah 53:5; Matthew 9:18-31; cf. 17:20-21; 8:16-17).

Another way our faith grows is through adversity. God upholds His children with His everlasting arms. Even when situations are not turning out the way that we hoped, we mature spiritually if we will allow God to be boss of our lives, and not us! "The eternal God is your refuge, and underneath are the everlasting arms; He will thrust out the enemy from before you" (Deuteronomy 33:27). Adversity will either make you bitter or better. The choice is yours! Which do you choose?

We are saved through faith. In Ephesians 2:8, God tells us, "For by grace are you saved through faith, and that not of yourselves; it is the gift of God not of works, lest anyone should boast."

Because we know and trust God does not mean that we will have a trouble-free life. No! We will all have trouble, whether we know God or not. Trouble is a fact of life. But God is interested in our response to that trouble. He will walk through trouble with us; in fact, most of the time, He will carry us through our troubles. Rest in God through the troubles of life. When the torrents of trouble are overwhelming on every side, and they are about to engulf you, ask God to throw His loving arms around you and embrace you. Then you will know and feel His comfort more than you could ever imagine. God allows affliction in our lives so that we can understand how to comfort others (2 Corinthians 1). God means for us to be able to comfort those around us also. As Paul went through severe trials for his faith, God also used him to go back and comfort those people who saw him suffering after God had given him divine comfort. Look around you and see the hurting people of our time and reach out to them.

Strengthen others with the same strength that God gives to each of us as we walk through dark days!

30

A Summer's Blaze

Summer arrived in the mountains in a beautiful way. One nice bene-fit here is that it is not as hot as other places in our state. Our motto for our county is "Where spring spends the summer." At our house, we live outside of town a fair distance so that our temperature is about ten degrees cooler than our town. After living at Hilton Head for the last eighteen years, it was a blessed relief.

Before we moved from Hilton Head, we had always wanted to live somewhere we could grow our own meat, have our own eggs, and possibly have our own cow for nice fresh organic milk. So we had been considering the prospects of purchasing a dairy cow.

George had lay hold of the fact of where one was available. After talking with the owner of the cow, George was excited that this farmer did not want money, but wanted George to bring chicken litter and spread it on his pastures in payment for the cow. We were excited as our finances were very low. This August morning seemed as though it was the day to ride to this farm to deliver this chicken fertilizer as the farmer had requested. We both went into our chicken houses to complete our daily chores.

One house was having some electrical problems when we turned on the electric feeder, and Bill, our friend, had already promised to come out on Saturday to fix the problem. As I again brought this to George's mind, he instructed me to leave it on for about an hour and then turn it off again. Then George left at about eleven o'clock with the spreader-truck full of chicken litter to deliver to the farmer that owned the cow.

The children and I all went into the house to fix a big meal for lunch that day. Each child had a job to prepare for this meal. As we were busily considering our own job, I looked out our side window at the beautiful summer day that lay before us. All of a sudden, my eye caught hold of the fact that I was seeing smoke passing through the air.

My mind went directly to the chicken house at the bottom of the hill that had the electrical problem. I ran as fast as I could toward it. When I reached the bottom of the hill, I saw that the whole house was enveloped in a very enormous cloud of smoke. My only thought was *Call the fire department!*

Our older son and daughter had followed me when I screamed that I saw smoke. Our son started to go inside when I yelled, "Don't do that!" He backed off and ran around the side of it to the back. He began throwing baby chicks into the yard by the handful. Every time he did, he reported later that they all ran back into the smoking building.

I ran back into the house to call the fire department! Our older daughter dashed back with me. I picked up the phone to dial and waited for an answer. When they answered, I was trying to tell them that our chicken house was on fire. They asked for our address. I was so flustered that I was not able to remember our new physical address. Our daughter grabbed the phone and explained it all to them perfectly. I was so thankful that she took charge.

Not only did she help with the phone, but she also sprinted barefoot down to our neighbor's house to tell him of our problem. She found him in his chicken house, and he immediately came up to help. Our daughter waited beside the road at his house to show the fire trucks exactly which house it was. They gave her a ride up the road to the correct location. It was necessary as we had eight houses over many acres of land.

When she arrived back home, she grabbed our camera and commenced to take pictures of the whole ordeal. Her dad had already told her that she was in charge of recording our journey on the farm through photography.

In the meantime, after calling the fire department, I told the younger children to stay in the house. I returned to the bottom of the hill to view this disastrous site. I started screaming my prayers to God. I poured out all my frustrations and thoughts concerning this matter. It was totally out of my hands. I was absolutely distraught beyond any normal limits.

"God, why did you allow this? We are now going to go under financially. God, help!" I kept pouring out my prayers and frustrations on the Lord in a violent way. I could imagine that we might even lose our whole farm from this fire.

Many neighbors arrived immediately as most of them were in the volunteer fire department. My prayers heightened as I saw them encircle the house and start to take stock of the situation. Many of them were trying to throw our furniture that was stored behind the chicken house out into the yard before it burned down. I was afraid for their lives, so I hollered to them to get away from that house. I would not have been able to stand the thought of one of them dying in that fire! My most earnest prayer of the day was "Lord, please keep everyone safe that no one would die today!"

One of the fears that was gripping me was the fact that one of the gas tanks that supplied each house's heat for the small chicks was located extremely close to the house that was on fire. There was only a one-way alley road between the house and the gas tank.

When the first trucks arrived from the fire house in our area, they ran to the house and immediately threw the two enormous front doors wide open. When they did, the entire house immediately burst into a blazing inferno. Fear ran through my entire being!

As ten different fire departments arrived in the trucks, they asked if there was a water supply. Because George had been the volunteer fire chief for the north end of Hilton Head, he had previously informed me that our pond outside by the house was a perfect fire hydrant if we ever had a fire. I quickly guided them to that area. They immediately set up to pump water into the fire from that pond.

The firemen and many of our neighbors all pitched in to help try to contain the fire. The fire became a furnace-like firestorm! I was very far away from it, but I could feel the intense hotness, as it began to melt the outside siding of the next chicken house, which was many feet away and slightly down the hill. It appeared as though the next house would burst into flames any minute. "How many houses would be lost because of this fire?" "Would we be able to rise above this disaster?" "Why did this have to happen when George is not here?"

"If the gas tank were to explode, what other tragedy would take place?" I contemplated. "Oh, God, please don't allow that gas tank to explode!" I shouted inside myself. The house was totally engulfed with flames, and it began to look like it was time for the charred boards to succumb to the fire's blast and fall to the ground. "Would it fall straight down on top of itself, or would it fall right onto that gas tank that is full of gas?" I shouted to the Lord. About that time, the house fell exactly on top of the gas tank!

I was anticipating a relentless fire that would also devour the next chicken house, for the tank was positioned compactly against the lower chicken house. Many of the firemen had already started drenching the roof with water several hours before this time to attempt to keep it from bursting into flames. "God save the next house and the men who were standing closely by it!"

By this time, several hours had elapsed since the firemen arrived to fight the blaze. Many women had come with their husbands to watch, and many were sitting on the hill where I was standing. They all heard all of my prayers, and they were experiencing the anguish of my heart, but not one of them ever embraced me or spoke a kind word to me. I suffered much anguish that day all alone. My heart felt as though I was all alone watching the tragedy of my life.

Have you ever felt as though you were so very alone in a harsh world with no one to comfort your hurts? I was painfully alone that day, even though I was surrounded with people, and George would not even be able to get home because of the traffic jam on our road. There was not any way to call him as cell phones were not yet invented.

Later George began to share with me how he felt when he returned to our community. The fire house in our section is at the end of Persimmon Road directly on the large highway. As he turned that corner, the first thing that hit him was the fact that all the fire trucks were gone. He then looked at the sky. It was thick with black smoke. His heart sank. He also remembered that we left on the feeder in the chicken house, and all promptly left to be about our other business.

His thoughts went directly to "It has to be my farm on fire!", "Is my family alright?" By the immensity of the smoke, he knew that it was a consuming fire that may have claimed many buildings, possibly including the house. He reported later that his heart cried out, "Why did I leave my family alone today!" This was actually the first time that He left us alone on the farm since we moved there. "Will I be able to get back to my family when I arrive there?" he contemplated as he drove closer to our farm.

As he drove up the road, he soon found that many trucks and cars were crowding the road so that he had to walk the rest of the way to find us. He was actually relieved when he realized that it was not our house and only one chicken house was burning and not all of the farm. By the immensity of this black smoke, he thought that the farm might be completely on fire.

Finally, I saw the most welcomed sight ever after all afternoon had already passed by. Praise God, it was George walking up the road. I ran to his arms, and he embraced me! I started bawling my eyes out. I started trying to explain what happened, but he hushed me and calmed me down by speaking loving words to me. I felt as though everything would be all right now, no matter what happened, for again we were reunited.

As he embraced me, I felt as though God were holding me and saying, "My child, it will be all right no matter how many houses burn down." God began to comfort me with the love that only He could give. When I was shouting at Him all afternoon, He still was loving me because God realizes that we are all made of dust (Psalm 103).

We are like the grass of the field, here today and gone tomorrow. But God is our Good Shepherd even in the midst of tragedy. He will never leave us alone or forsake us.

For many weeks after the fire, I was having nightmares about it. That summer, our house did not have any air-conditioning, so the windows were open all day and all night. This fire was still smoldering many weeks after that day. When the wind shifted, the smoke blew into the house, and just the smell brought back horrible memories of that fateful day. At night, it caused me to relive that day all over again. I would wake up in panic. Finally, the smoke was quenched, and all was well.

Now I pray for people whose houses burned down. I pray that our family would never have to experience this kind of tragedy ever again.

"Thank you, God, that the gas tank never exploded and caused the other chicken house to burst into flames. Thank you, God, also that no man was killed in our fire. You are so very gracious to us!"

> Praise Your name, Oh Lord, "we went through the fire and the water, yet You brought us out into a place of abundance" (Psalm 66:12).

> Come and hear, all who fear God, and I will tell of what He has done for my soul. I cried to Him with my mouth, and He was extolled with my tongue . . . But certainly God has heard; He has given heed to the voice of my prayer. Blessed be God, who has not turned away my prayer nor His loving kindness from me. (Psalm 66:16–17, 19–20)

> The Lord reigns, let the peoples tremble; He is enthroned above the cherubim. Let the earth shake! The Lord is great in Zion. And He is exalted above all the peoples. Let them praise Your great and awesome name; Holy is He. Exalt the Lord our God and worship at His footstool; Holy is He. (Psalm 99:1–3, 5)

Some of us have to walk in many paths of life, but God is in all those paths. Some will experience fire as we did, but others will experience water tragedy, and some will experience the loss of loved ones, but all of us will be saved from our tragedies through His blood.

His blood washes us clean from our sin. It protects us from Satan, and it secures our place in heaven with God. If it were not for the blood of Jesus, we would not have our inheritance in His kingdom. His blood is on the mercy seat of God in heaven where it ever pleads for our soul. It is the satisfaction for our sin, and when the Father sees His Son's blood, His anger is abated against us because Jesus died for our sins by nailing them to His Cross. Jesus bore the anger of the Father against sin for us so that we would never have to experience that. Praise His name!

God is so good even when we go through mighty trials. He carries us in His arms of love! His grace is always sufficient for us (2 Corinthians 12:9). "So, do not worry about tomorrow; for tomorrow, will care for itself. Each day has enough trouble of its own" (Matthew 6:34).

Here is a foot note to this story that was discovered 31 years after this fire. In the early spring of 2017, George had to repair a hole in the roof of the chicken house that was closest to the one that burned. The siding of this house had melted during the fire.

As he tore off the tin from the roof, the rafters under it were charred and black. This showed him that this house was within minutes of bursting into flames the day that the other house burned down. Thank you, God that You stayed the fire and did not allow it to consume the second house even though we did not realize it at the time.

This is a picture of the chicken house that had already burned down. The feeder and the door into the foot washing room were still standing. The gas tanks located on the edge of the road miraculously did not explode. The chicken house, while burning, collapsed into that small driveway next to the gas tanks. The chicken house on the level below had its siding melted on that side. As you can see, many structures were within a few feet of this house.

31

With God, Closed Doors Open!

Now it was two days after the chicken house fire when George went to pick up our cow that he had promised to buy from that farmer that fateful day. I thought, "Could anything else happen while he would be gone?"

About an hour after he drove away, the children and I were in the house preparing lunch. All of a sudden, the alarms that are on the chicken houses sounded. It was as if a Calvary were being summoned to battle. Every house has a siren that resonates piercingly through the air. We all jumped a mile because all seven houses sounded together.

This alarm was a very serious action because this meant that all electric power to the farm has ceased, and it will only be minutes before the chickens will start to die. All the children and myself scampered and dashed to the duty of opening up the enormous doors on the front and the back of the chicken houses. Under normal circumstances, they would be difficult to open for an adult and impossible to open for children.

Large chickens occupied three of the houses at the lower end of the farm. The other four houses were inhabited with young chickens. As we were scampering our friend, Chuck, arrived in the nick of time. He ran with our younger children to help them to unfasten those enormous doors.

I went directly to the houses that had almost grown chickens. Those houses were more critical to open first, as it would only be seconds before the larger chickens would die when the fans ceased to function. It was amazing how fast the heat intensity rose with twenty-thousand larger chickens in one house.

I scurried down the road to the lower three houses first. Each door on the front and back of every house seemed as though it weighed a ton, as I pressed hard against them to unfasten them. The heat intensity in those houses was mounting every second! A blast of hot air would slap me in the face with every door opening!

When I completed the houses that had larger chickens, I worked my way to the houses where the smaller chickens were. The children and Chuck had already opened every door. We had all scurried around in about an hour, making sure that we had completed all of our tasks.

After realizing that there was not anything else that needed to be done, we all fell to the ground under our large trees and were resting in the coolness of the grass. A luscious breeze passed over our overheated bodies. Even though it was the hottest part of the day, we felt a relief from the heat as we lay there resting.

Not long after we were resting, George came home with the cow. He found Chuck, our friend, the children, and myself all stretched out on the ground in our front yard. His questions were "What are you doing? Are you all right?" No! I replied. We had a power failure! My next response was "You better not leave us alone on this farm by ourselves anymore!"

Within a two-day period, we experienced a major disaster of a burning chicken house and a potential disaster with the power failure. Praise God, He saw us through both successfully!

Again, I would have to say, "*But God!*" God always lights our way even in the darkest forest of life, and He opens the doors of life for us. He literally opened those doors for us as they were extremely heavy even for me, much less the children. Every door was opened extremely rapidly even by the children and our friend. We did not lose any chickens from the heat. As soon as the doors were opened, the cool breeze started drawing through those houses straightway!

"For You are my lamp, O Lord; and the Lord illumines my darkness." Those chickens that day were sitting in darkness in the heat of the day, but God delivered them before they died . . . He is a tower of deliverance and shows loving kindness to His anointed (2 Samuel 22:29, 51). Praise His name!

Praise His name that His eye is always on His children. He sees our problems and enters our life to make a way of escape. In 1 Corinthians 10:13, God reminds us, "No temptation has overtaken you but such is common to man; and God is faithful, who will not allow you to be tempted beyond what you are able, but with the temptation will provide the way of escape also, so that you will be able to endure it". Praise His wonderful name!

32

God's Indescribable Blessings

Our fifth child was born almost three years after we moved to Clayton from Hilton Head. We moved to the mountains in January 1986, and neither one of us were necessarily thinking about having another child. We thought that our family was complete, but all of sudden, we both had a desire to have another child. However, there were two miscarriages before I became pregnant with Michael. God had another plan, and Michael was on his way after Mom and Dad had a very special night together in early spring of 1988.

God had given me a strong desire to become pregnant with another child, but I was very nervous about whether I would be able to hold this child since I had lost two previously. The other two pregnancies had been about three months, and they were very harsh. I did not look forward to having that happen again.

I went to the doctor when I was about six weeks pregnant, and the doctor did an ultrasound to make sure the baby was alive. Oh, how wonderful when I saw Michael for the very first time, the bag was pulsating regularly with each heartbeat. I was ecstatic that he was alive, and I was truly going to have another child even when I was forty-two years old.

The early part of the pregnancy went well. I was able to hold him without any bleeding until I returned for my visit when I was three months. At this time, I was examined, and the doctor reported that I had dilated to one at only three months. This was terrifying news. "How was I going to be able to hold this child for another six months?" I thought. In order to hold this pregnancy, my doctor said that we would have to stitch my cervix closed, as I had to do with most of the other pregnancies.

At three months, she put the stitch in my cervix but could not tighten it to the closed position because it probably would cause me to go into labor and have this child. She secured it at the position of one and sent me home. I was excited that it was holding, and I was not having any symptoms of losing him any longer.

I had a normal pregnancy for the first seven months. Since we had high-school-age as well as elementary-age children, I was a very busy mother. I always took all the children to the sports games of the older two children. They participated in cross-country, basketball, and track. We all went to the out-of-town games as well.

One fall morning when I was taking Deena to school, I was listening to the radio and singing with it. All of a sudden, I had an awful thought that something was wrong with our baby. I was in tears when I returned home. I began trying to deal with the idea that this baby was not normal. It was a hard struggle. I prayed that our baby would not have Down's syndrome. My doctor performed a high quality ultrasound because of my age. I told her not to tell me the results. That was for her information, and I would wait until the child was born to see the baby's condition.

Eddie entered college in the fall of 1988 at Asbury College in Wilmore, Kentucky. He participated in cross-country there. So off to the college campus we went for a parent's weekend. It was a very special time with many activities, and we enjoyed all the festivities that weekend.

Upon returning home, I started having labor pains and had to go to bed. When my doctor examined me, she immediately reported that I would have to remain in bed without getting up except for short times. I was given medication to stop the contractions. This occurred on the last day of October 1988. He was not due until the day after Christmas. So I had to look forward to being in the bed all of the month of November and most of December. This was horrible news because we had three children at home—Deena was sixteen, David was ten, Rachel was eight. I was homeschooling the younger two, and Deena was a junior at Rabun Gap-Nachoochee School.

I slept most of the time when it first started because the medication made me very drowsy. As the weeks went on, I was able to cut back on the medication to stop the labor. I was very bored, so I told David and Rachel to bring me drawers, and I cleaned out every drawer in the house from my bed. I really had to be bored if I was cleaning out drawers. Since that was all I could do, I kept busy for a few days in between homeschooling. I was very thankful that David and Rachel were old enough to do their schoolwork with very little prompting.

An interesting occurrence happened every Sunday. I would always have severe labor pains and had to return to the medication. There was not even one Sunday that I was free of labor pains. I thought that one Sunday would be His birthday, and sure enough it was. Michael was born on Sunday, December 11, 1988.

I was awakened on this particular Sunday at four o'clock in the morning. My abdomen was hard as a rock. Even though I had experienced labor on every Sunday for the last six weeks, my abdomen had never been hard like that on any Sunday before this one. My doctor had a special medicine that I was to take if I thought that I was truly in labor to test if it was true or false labor. I took the medication and returned to sleep. I woke up several hours later, and I was still having contractions. Even though I was in true labor, my husband took the children and went to church that Sunday. My contractions were steady but not extremely close together. I was alone for several hours. When the family returned from church, they fixed lunch, and all was well except for labor pains that were increasing.

The other complication of that day was the fact that we had chickens going to market that night. What were we going to do with having an all-night ordeal with them going to market?

I had thought that I would be able to not have the baby that day because I managed to rest through the other labors on every other Sunday. I also wanted to study chemistry with our older daughter, as she was having a major test on that Monday. After lunch, my husband went out to begin to get the chickens ready for market. Our oldest son went with him so that George could explain all that would need to be done before the catchers came that evening. My neighbor came to visit with me during those hours. The labor pains were increasing with severity and frequency. I told my neighbor to go tell George that he needed to come home no matter what was happening. As she was going to get him, he came home and called the doctor.

The doctor said to come immediately. I tried to remind her that we live more than an hour away from the hospital, but she hung up before I was able to say that. But George had to go through all the activities that Eddie needed to do that evening before the catchers came for the chickens. This was major, leaving Eddie, who was only seventeen years old, with all the duties that needed to be done. He had never helped his dad before in this process. But there was not anything that we could do differently. We left fairly quickly for the hospital, but we had a leisurely ride there since I had not been out to enjoy the Christmas lights and even enjoy the outside scenery in so many weeks.

When we arrived at the hospital, I was sent immediately to surgery because I still had my stitch in place, and they could not remove it at that point. The doctor and the staff at the hospital thought that I had gone to a closer hospital because my uterus had a possibility of rupturing, but of course, we did not know that.

A cesarean section was done because he was breech, and the stitch could not be removed. I was highly upset by that decision. I had a spinal and was awake during this surgery. It was wild! I felt as though I could feel somewhat, and I kept telling everyone that I could feel that. They laughed because they pulled the baby out at that moment. Praise God! It was over.

At birth, Michael was a strapping little football player. He was very muscular with a broad chest. He looked as though he were ready to take on anybody. He was handsome and very well-built. George said that when the pediatrician took him to the nursery, he showed him off to many people because he was particularly tough-looking. Everything seemed to be well.

He started to nurse shortly after birth and nursed aggressively. Praise God! All systems seemed to be working well. We went home three days after his birth with an appointment to return in two weeks to the pediatrician.

We were so excited that we had a normal, healthy baby. When we went to the doctor in two weeks, he told us that Michael had a heart murmur. He sent him to Emory to be tested for a possible hole in his heart.

After being checked out by the specialist at Emory University, he discussed the possibility that he had a medium-sized hole in his heart. Every time the valve would open, it closed this hole up temporarily. It was only open when the valve was shut. That was good because it did not have as much blood flowing back into the other chamber as would have happened if it were in another location.

After being on a heart medication for one month, we returned for another checkup. The doctor took him off any heart medication and told us to watch out for certain symptoms, but he did not have to see him anymore unless he had trouble.

The pediatrician suspected Down's syndrome because of the hole in the heart. I was devastated with this news! I struggled much with the thought that my child was not normal. I rocked him often and prayed through many tears that God would heal him. But God said "No!" because nothing was changing. I had a very difficult time accepting that he would not have a typical life. But God was so faithful in that it could have been much worse. He developed much more quickly than any child with Down's syndrome.

After testing at about three years of age, we were told that he was a mosaic of Down's syndrome even though this is very rare. The tests revealed he was one-third Down's, one-third normal, and one-third something that they did not have a name for yet. They explained that when the normal cells were developing, he would act brighter, and when the Down's cells were progressing he would be less bright. We found this to be true.

Furthermore, when he approached his third birthday, we became concerned about school. All our other children had either attended a Christian school or was homeschooled, but this would not be possible with Michael.

We considered the possibility that we would place him in public school. When he was one and a half years old, he became blind because of congenital cataracts. George had been born with them also, but they were not diagnosed until he was fifty years old. George had problems reading in school, but no one realized that his problem was cataracts in his eyes. These particular cataracts only produced small dots on the lens that would block out certain words. So George would skip certain words when he was reading.

When Michael was tested, it was shown that he was experiencing the exact type of cataracts that his dad experienced even as a young child. Michael was only three years old when his cataracts completely occluded his vision. He had his first cataract removed at that time. We saw a pediatric ophthalmologist at Emory University.

One day I saw Eddie, who was seventeen years old at this time. He was standing in the middle of the dining room like a straight stick not moving at all. I walked by and asked, "What are you doing?" He replied that he was playing hide-and-seek with Michael. It was really sad when the children wanted to play with Michael, and they did not have to hide at all. "Mom, we figured out that if we stand completely still, Michael will not see us," Eddie explained.

When the doctor diagnosed the problem and told us that he would have to remove the lens as you would in an older person, I kept asking him, "How many children have you done that were Michael's age?"

He would always reply, "I have done ninety-nine baby monkey eyes."

I would always say to George on the way home that he never answers my question. When the day came for Michael's surgery on his first eye, I decided that I would ask this question one more time!

Michael was prepared for surgery, and we did not see the doctor until after that surgery. When he came to give us a report about Michael's condition, I said, "You never answer my question about how many children's eyes you have done. Today, I want to get a straight answer from you. How many children's lens have you removed in each eye at such a young age?"

He replied, "Michael is the very first child who I have had to remove cataracts in both eyes."

I am presenting Michael's case, and I am doing a study on him since this is something that is highly unusual. After the surgery, Michael could see very quickly. He followed Michael until he was about twenty years old.

Life is full of surprises, but God is always with you every step of the way. God says "I will never leave you, nor forsake you (Hebrews 13:5; cf. Psalm 27:7–9; 38:21–22). God has a purpose for every child who is born, whether he is normal or has severe problems. There is a specific purpose, and we all need to look beyond the dark cloud in our life to discover the silver lining of that same cloud. I know that every tear I have cried over Michael and the thought that he would never be normal, God knows. God has "put my tears into His bottle; are they not in Your book?" (Psalm 56:8). God remembers our sufferings!

Even though God allows "great and severe troubles" in our life, He will "revive us again from the depths of the earth." Also, He will "increase our greatness and comfort us on every side" (Psalm 71:19–21). Did you see that through trials, God will increase our greatness? Trials bring us closer to God and will either make us better or bitter.

It is only "through the loving kindness of the Most-High, I will not be shaken!" (Psalm 21:7). God will keep my feet on a solid foundation, the "Rock", and will not allow the storms of life to sweep me away (Matthew 7:24–25; Psalm 71:3, 7b). "I will go in the strength of the Lord God" (Psalm 71:16). "God will deliver the needy when he cries" (Psalm 72:12).

Michael was and continues to be a wonderful blessing to us day by day! God knew what we needed!

Michael now is 28 years old and thriving. He is still doing his homeschool, but without me prompting him. He has a program on his computer where the teacher teaches the lessons and he does the work in the workbook. I do not have to teach him at all anymore.

Michael is working independently of me completely. He loves his school work and thrives on it. He thinks of it as his job. When I say "Help, me clean the house" or ask him if he wants to go with me to town, he will say he has to do his school work.

He is now much taller than both of us. He is at least 5 feet 10 inches or more. He looks like a linebacker for any football team. He is extremely strong and muscular. There is not anything wimpy about Michael. His brothers-in-law hand fight with him for fun. I usually say, "Michael don't hurt them". He is stronger than any of them. He is our helper in the house and on the farm.

He is absolutely one of God's special blessings for us. He keeps us feeling young and active.

How about you? What kind of stories do you have that God has presented to you and your family?

You need to consider the hand of God in your life. He reveals Himself to all who obey His Word (John 14:15–21). Remember obedience does not win salvation, but it is evidence of the believer's love for God. We obey those we truly love.

John MacArthur makes this statement about the place of obedience and works in the life of a believer. "Jesus emphasized the need for the habitual practice of obedience to His commands as evidence of the believer's love for Him and the Father. This is consistent with the teachings of James 2:14–26 that true saving faith is manifested by works produced by God in the transforming, regenerating power of the Spirit. Those works are expressions of the love which the Spirit pours into the believer's heart (Romans 5:5; Galatians 5:22)." Allow God to pour into your life and heart to allow you to write down the stories of your life.

This is one way that you can reach many people, that you will never meet, with the gospel of the Lord Jesus Christ. You could have an opportunity to *speak* into their lives and to *win fruit* for God's glory so that you can bear much fruit in your life (John 15).

This is a picture of Michael when he was about five years old.

33

As For God, His Ways Are Perfect!

On Friday, March 19, 2017 we received news that our close friend had cancer. His doctor told him after doing a CT scan that he had fourth stage cancer. I was so struck by this news, that I set aside the whole day to pray and ask God what message would He give to this hurting family.

I began to write how God has all of us in a "school of faith" most of our lives. He is allowing many types of hardships to cross our paths and build our faith in Him. As I was contemplating what to say to our friends, I began to write what was my largest problem when struck with a storm in life.

My response inside of myself, in the past, has been to believe what others say to me instead of relying on who God is and what He says in His Word. It was not always visible on the outside, but my inner most thoughts were completely torn apart. I found myself writing what I needed to hear.

I will have to say when most people are confronted with a diagnosis of fourth stage cancer, they will tend to believe in circumstances and negative thoughts from others rather than allowing faith in God to rule their situation. This is a devastating thought to be able to process successfully.

We need to *not* believe the *facts by sight,* but rely on the *facts by faith* in a powerful, all knowing God. Many times in our life, God has turned around the facts by sight. Many facts in life may be true, but God has the final word as to what will be the truth by faith.

I wrote the majority of that day and then delivered this letter at five o'clock in the afternoon when his wife was off from work. We sat and talked and shared many thoughts together. God strengthens both parties when we consider who God is and how Almighty and powerful He is.

As I contemplated what I should say to a hurting couple and family, I thought about how God caused my faith to soar in Him when I am in His Word every day. I would meditate, memorize, and apply His Word to my life. I began to go through what I had written in this book as applications to these stories. One particular application came to mind.

Faith is the absence of fear! Wow! What a thought! Did I really believe this or was this just a trite statement that just rolls off my tongue when someone else was hurting and not myself? Could I really hang onto God even when I was, again, confronted with the severe news of having an even more deadly kind of cancer?

That afternoon, my friend and I had a wonderful time sharing our thoughts of God. Trying to uplift each other and cause our faith in God to rise to even higher limits. As I drove home, my faith, as hers, was flying high. We both knew that our God was in control and He allowed certain things for a purpose.

On Saturday, I studied the Bible to even gain a greater understanding of needing to trust in God, especially when the chips were down and our life was in turmoil. We, all, need to realize that no one truly knows what a day will bring forth.

By Sunday morning on the way to church, I was discussing out loud with my husband all of the things that I had discovered and reminded myself of how we need to respond to tribulations. I was *flying high in my faith in God.* Of course, our life was on the upswing and it was our friend that was having these trials.

Even when church was over that day, we went out to eat with several of our friends. After this wonderful dinner and fellowship, I went to the rest room. From that moment on, our life turned from walking on cloud nine to wondering what would happen next. Sometimes I wonder how things can be so wonderful and in the course of a few minutes be devastating. By the time, we returned home in a thirty-minute period, I knew that something horrible could be coming.

In the middle of Sunday afternoon, I began having female problems to disturbing proportions. I called my doctor and he gave me medication to try to stop this from happening. He told me to stay in bed and call him first thing Monday morning.

At about eleven o'clock at night when I had already been asleep for about an hour, George woke me up when he was coming to bed. I turned over and reached out for him and quietly said, "Something is not right!"

At that moment, I knew that the flood gates had been released. I was hemorrhaging and for ten minutes it continued to extremely alarming proportions. I was *beside myself* when I realized what was taking place. I screamed out to God, "Help me!" I could not think straight at that moment. I relied on George to tell me what to do.

He, immediately, helped me to get ready to go the emergency room. After arriving there, the hemorrhaging slowed down, but did not stop for two and a half weeks. It was at alarming proportions, but not devastating. The doctor requested a CT scan to determine the exact cause of this episode. The cervix was determined to be of most concern.

The doctor in the emergency room, as soon as he received the results of the scan, came to us to report the findings. I was totally struck by the way that he presented this news. He had the biggest smile on his face that he could have had when he spoke these words, "You have a ninety-nine percent chance of having cancer."

Since I was more upset by the way he presented this news to us, I responded with "O.K." I could have cared less that night what he said, because how he said it was very disturbing to me. He seemed to have no regard for our feelings in this matter. I believe that he was reviewing my intense history with cancer over almost the past seven years, and he realized that I had not done what the doctors recommended then. He seemed to be pleased to tell the "great news" that I had only a one percent chance of not having cancer. His bedside manner was completely lacking in the middle of that night.

Another test that was completed so that they would be able to pinpoint the problem more exactly was an ultra sound. We left the hospital before the results of that test were available. By this time, it was five o'clock Monday morning. We were extremely tired. We returned home at six-thirty in the morning. George only got about an hour or so of sleep that night and had to start the next day. He had several surgeries with his client's animals scheduled for that Monday plus walk-in patients all afternoon.

When I awoke that morning after resting from a turbulent night, I began to try to get an appointment with the doctor that the hospital recommended that night. I tried to talk with his receptionist, but only received a voice mail. I, then, called my doctor that had given me the medicine on Sunday afternoon. He called the same doctor that I had tried to call and they told him that I would have to wait in order to see him.

The nurse of the doctor that had given me the medicine on Sunday found me another doctor that was able to see me within two days. After seeing this second doctor, we were told that I would have to go through another test to determine exactly what it was. The first two tests were inconclusive.

My gynecologist added that when he reviewed the results of the first two tests, it looked very suspicious for cancer. A week later, I went back to the hospital to complete this next test. The anesthetic seemed to depress me greatly. As soon as I awoke, my eyes kept weeping when I did not know why I was crying.

In order to overcome this depression that lasted about three days, I kept my I-phone on my favorite Christian music to be able to function. When we are singing the high praises of God on our lips and have the Sword of the Spirit (Word of God) in our hand, we will not be depressed (Psalm 149:6; cf. Hebrews 4:12). Praise God!

Furthermore, I was hearing from God with *rhemas* from His Word. The first was Deuteronomy 32:4, "God is my Rock; His work is perfect; for all His ways are justice, a God of truth and without injustice; Righteous and upright is He."

I kept repeating this verse that God is my rock, His ways are perfect, and He is a faithful God who is righteous, true, and just. My heart was trying to cave in to the words of the doctors, but my faith kept rising up within me commanding me to remember what a wonderful God I have. I will have to say, I struggled many times, but never completely gave in with negative thoughts.

I kept remembering that the fall of 2017 would be seven years since God showed me His perfect will for me concerning cancer. My prayer at that time was "God, if you don't want me to do the chemotherapy, please shut the door!" He literally shut the door. For details see the story called, *Life is an Exhilarating Whirlwind!* This story is number one in this book.

I have been faithful to this program for the most part. I will continue this protocol for the rest of my life.

Another *rhema* that God gave me during this test was Psalm 91:14-16. "Because he has set his love upon Me, therefore I will deliver him; I will set him on high, because he has known My name. He shall call upon Me, and I will answer him; I will be with him in trouble; I will deliver him and honor him. With long life, I will satisfy him. And show him My salvation."

Jesus is right there with us in all situations. "He will never leave us or forsake us" (Hebrews 13:5). He will always give us a way of escape in temptations and trials (1 Corinthians 10:13).

This is the third time that a doctor has tried to tell me that I have a reoccurring cancer. The first time was not of any significance, but the doctor's words were, "This is probably the cancer returning." The symptoms soon disappeared and nothing had to be done.

The second-time recurring cancer was mentioned was frightening. I was in a doctor's office talking about fixing two disc in my neck. When that doctor took an x-ray of my neck, she discovered gray matter on my spinal cord. She was greatly alarmed and reported that it was probably cancer. She went so far as to say that the cancer was probably in the brain also. After doing a CT scan with contrast, she found out that it was nothing. But that time for an entire week, we both were greatly unnerved. We did not share with our children, but kept this quiet until we knew for sure. That was a couple of years ago.

So when the third time happened a few weeks ago, the doctors saw what they were calling cancer and they jumped to conclusions immediately. The emergency doctor reported ninety-nine percent chance of cancer. Even my gynecologist reported to me after review-ing the films, "It does not look good."

Another week went by before obtaining the results. My doctor first stated that he had good news. I stopped and out loud praised God. He agreed with me. He stated, "There were NO CANCER cells!" The cervix was reported to be chronically irritated, but no cancer. Lord, You are so very good!

When he gave me the good report of no cancer on April 6, he commented that he did not understand this. The lesion was believed to be cancerous, but no cancer cells were found. Praise God from whom all blessings flow!

Everyone needs to realize that cancer goes through every one's body from time to time. If you have a good immune system, your body will throw it off.

I believe that cancer tried to come, but was thrown off due to the good cancer protocol that God had previously shown me.

One of the names for God is Jehovah-Rapha, the God who heals. This concept was first shown to man in Exodus 15:26, "For I am the Lord who heals." (Exodus 23:25; Deuteronomy 32:39; 1 Samuel 2:6; Psalm 41:3-4, 68:20, 103:3, 147:30; cf. Isaiah 53:5).

Healing comes from God alone! Whether we go to the doctor or a pastor for direction, healing stills comes from God. God gives doctors wisdom to do the techniques that they perform. I am very thankful for doctors, but we need to realize that God grants them healing for their patients whether they recognize it or not.

We need to realize that *not* all the procedures done by doctors support the God-given healing process. Sometimes their medica-tions will inhibit this process. An example of this is when doctors use chemotherapy, this destroys your natural immune system which is needed to properly fight the cancer. That is why so many people have infections of all sorts while using this method. Many of them have to be hospitalized and some die from run-away infections that have nothing to do with the cancer. With a destroyed immune system, they do not have a chance of surviving.

Chemotherapy, also, makes one's body acidic on the PH scale. Cancer thrives in an acidic body. After having one chemotherapy, my body was so very acidic that it took me six months for my body to become alkalized to a cancer killing range.

Furthermore, radiation burns the good cells as well as the cancerous ones. It does permanent damage to the body that does not have anything to do with the cancer process. This damage cannot be reversed.

It was God who set me thinking in alternative ways or "thinking out of the box". My dad had died from his first chemotherapy treatment many years before this time. I had said, at that time, "I will never do chemotherapy." His blood dropped to alarming proportions and never returned to normal. He died a little time later. When I experienced the effects of chemotherapy through my dad, I knew there had to be a better way.

My program for cancer has several elements. The first book that God gave me that supports the body's natural healing process was by Bill Henderson, *How to Cure Almost Any Kind of Cancer for $5.15/day at Home.* Here is a simple outline:

1. It is important that our immune system is working properly in order to fight cancer. People with cancer do not have much of an immune system that is working. That is why they have cancer. Poor nutrition, which can lead to infection in the gums, mouth, or teeth, and environmental pollutants are some of the reasons for a faulty immune system.

A proper immune system is vital to causing the body to heal from the cancer. I take a product that causes my immune system to work properly every day. Furthermore, good quality vitamin and mineral supplements are a must to support your immune system, as well as a diet rich in vegetables and other green, leafy foods.

2. The shake I drink every morning basically feeds the cells with extra oxygen. When you have cancer, the cells are shut off from taking in oxygen. Cancer is anaerobic which means that it does not allow cells to open up to oxygen any longer. To simplify this process, the shake mixture that Mr. Henderson recommends causes the cells to open and take in the needed oxygen which kills the cancer.

This shake also contains needed oils that our body requires for health. It is a high dose of this important oil. Also, in this shake are fruits that will alkalize your body when consumed.

3. When we have cancer, our body is acidic on the PH scale. Usually, it will register about 5.5 in PH. Cancer thrives in an acidic body. When we eat foods that are alkaline in nature, this causes our acidity to rise to the alkalized range. Cancer cannot thrive in an alkalized body. Mr. Henderson recommends an easy way to check every day where your body registers on the PH scale.

Diet is highly important in fighting cancer. Products made with white flour, sugar, caffeine, and processed foods are out of the question. We must eat an abundance of fresh, leafy vegetables.

4. Essiac Tea is necessary to eradicate cancer. This formula for the tea was first used by a home health nurse, Renee Caisse, and she had obtained this information from the Indians to whom she ministered in Canada. The Indians reported that this would cure anything. She started out with a four-herb formula. Today, it is currently composed of eight herbs that when combined together, will kill the cancer cells.

5. Proper amounts of iodine have a huge effect on curing cancer. The statistics show us that ninety-five percent

of Americans are low in iodine due to our diet. David Brownstein, M.D, has a book about this subject. See the list of books below.

This test that I have just completed proved that this protocol works in killing cancer. All the evidence of cancer was there--a lesion, except for the cancer cells.

I give God alone all the glory for this healing! He is the Almighty, merciful, gracious, powerful God who reigns above anything doctors want to tell you. He showed me this protocol and His ways are perfect!

There are many books on the market today that speak of healing cancer the natural way. Some of these authors are Bill Henderson, *How to Cure Almost Any Kind of Cancer for $5.15/day at Home* and also *Cancer Free: Your Guide to Gentle, Non-Toxic Healing.* The first book is the one that a friend sent to me. It is such easy reading with many wonderful testimonies in it. It laid out an easy to follow cancer program. Mr. Henderson spent many years researching a better way to cure cancer rather than radiation and chemotherapy. His own testimony about cancer, through his wife, is given in this book.

Ty Bollinger's dad had an aggressive kind of cancer and six other family members died with cancer in about a 10 year period. This set him on a quest to find answers about cancer. He has now written several books. Two of his lastest books are— *The 31 Day Guide to Gentle, Non-Toxic Healing,* and *The Truth about Cancer.*

Carolyn Gross wrote *Treatable and Beatable: Healing Cancer Without Surgery.* Also, Carolyn Gross and Geronimo Rubio, M.D. team up to write *Breaking the Cancer Code: A Revolutionary Approach to Reversing Cancer.*

This next book will tell you about Essiac Tea--*Canada's Remarkable Unknown Cancer Remedy: The Essiac Report* by Richard Thomas.

Another element in healing cancer involves iodine. David Brownstein wrote a book, *Iodine: Why You Can't Live Without It.* He tells of the wonderful effects of iodine on cancer.

Remember, we need to first run to God for answers when we are sick. Today, most people run to doctors rather than to God. God is the One who heals, and He imparts wisdom and knowledge to people if they will listen, but not all doctors are in touch with God.

It seems as though drug companies control the doctors as to what procedures to use for healing. Drugs, many times, inhibit the body's God-given healing process. Several drugs can interact in such a way that they cause more problems rather than encourage healing. Learn to study and research your own information about what you will allow doctors to do or what they will give you.

Come to know God so that you will be able to hear Him speak to you through His Word, through circumstances of life, and through other godly people. His Word is our best guide in life. He will impart truth and knowledge to you about any situation if you will seek His face (Psalm 27:4-5, 8, 14; 34:7-10; 63:1-5; 105:1-5; 119:2, 45; cf. 14:2). Rely on Him for answers.

Having an open and close relationship with God and obedience to His Word are the two main pre-requisites for hearing from God. Sin in our lives must be confessed and turned from, and we should apply His Word to our life and obey it (John 14:21).

Jesus talks about the cost of discipleship in Luke 9:23-26. First, we must deny ourselves and allow Jesus to take rule in our life. Our lives need to be lived for His will, not our will. We can never be ashamed of Him before men. We are to stick so close to Jesus as a branch abides in the vine (John 15:4-5, 7). Secondly, we are to bear much fruit in order to be His disciple (vv.8, 16). Thirdly, we are to love God above all others, and love others as much as we love ourselves (vv. 9-10, 13-14; 1 John 4:12-16). When we do these things, we will have the joy of the Lord (John 15:11) and God will manifest Himself to us.

1. What is the most fun activity that you or your family has ever done? Describe how you felt as God unfolded this incredible story? What did God do to make it so much fun and worthwhile to benefit you or your family? How did each member feel about this activity?

    _____

    _____

    _____

2. What is the most devastating event in your life? How did God make a way of escape for you? How did you feel while walking through this event? What did God teach you through this situation?

    _____

    _____

    _____

3. What is the most rewarding moment of your life? Why was it rewarding? What things of eternal value came out of this time?

    _____

    _____

    _____

4. What would you repeat in your life should you ever have an opportunity?

    _____

    _____

    _____

5. What would you change in your life if you could?

_____

_____

_____

6. What regrets do you have about your life?

_____

_____

_____

7. What do you believe God wants you to do in this life and why?

_____

_____

_____

These questions are for you contemplate how God has led you and entered into your life through many years. Use them as a springboard to write down your times where God has led you as a shepherd and gave you your answer to the storms of life.

ABOUT THE AUTHOR

Marywinn R. Lent graduated from Savannah High School in 1963 where she had been a majorette for three years. She spent the first twenty-one years as single in Savannah, and at the University of Georgia, where she encountered the love of her life, George Lent. She met him in May and they married in December 1966. She graduated from UGA with a BS in education with a major in speech therapy, and George graduated with a doctorate in veterinary medicine. After graduating from college, George and Marywinn moved to Hilton Head Island in June 1968 where he was the first veterinarian. They have five children of their own. After spending two years in Russia, their five Russian orphans came to live with them for nine summers on their farm in the Smoky Mountains. Furthermore, while in Russia, they met a Liberian daughter who resided with them for five years while she was in college. They currently have seventeen biological grandchildren with another six "adopted in their heart grandchildren" from their Russian and Liberian children. They would like to share part of their lives with you in order to bring glory to God.